Methuen Drama Modern Classics

The Methuen Drama Modern Plays series has always been at the forefront of modern playwriting and has reflected the most exciting developments in modern drama since 1959. To commemorate the fiftieth anniversary of Methuen Drama, the series was relaunched in 2009 as Methuen Drama Modern Classics, and continues to offer readers a choice selection of the best modern plays.

The Accrington Pals

'Like all Whelan's best work, the piece is blessed with a warm unsentimental humanity, but there is toughness too, in his chronicle of the terrible waste of war, and in the tensions of class and ideals, between a group of characters we come to care about deeply. There is no mistaking the play's power, intelligence and compassion.'

Daily Telegraph

Peter Whelan was born in the Potteries in 1931. His plays include *Captain Swing* (RSC The Other Place, 1978), *The Accrington Pals* (RSC Pit, 1981), *Clay* (RSC Pit, 1983), *The Bright and Bold Design* (RSC Pit, 1991), *The School of Night* (RSC The Other Place, 1992), *Shakespeare Country* (Little Theatre Guild, 1993), *The Tinderbox* (New Vic, 1994), *Divine Right* (Birmingham Rep, 1996), *The Herbal Bed* (RSC The Other Place, 1996, West End and New York), *Overture* (New Vic, 1997), *Nativity* (with Bill Alexander, Birmingham Rep, 1999), *A Russian in the Woods* (RSC, 2001) and *The Earthly Paradise* (Almeida, 2004). His work for television includes *The Trial of Lord L_____* and _____ tances. He is married, has t_____ s in London.

Peter Whelan

The Accrington Pals

with an introduction by
John Davey

B L O O M S B U R Y
LONDON · NEW DELHI · NEW YORK · SYDNEY

Bloomsbury Methuen Drama

An imprint of Bloomsbury Publishing Plc

50 Bedford Square	1385 Broadway
London	New York
WC1B 3DP	NY 10018
UK	USA

www.bloomsbury.com

Bloomsbury is a registered trade mark of Bloomsbury Publishing PLC

First published by Methuen London Ltd in 1982
This edition first published by Methuen Drama in 2011
Reprinted 2012, 2013 (twice), 2014

© Peter Whelan 1982, 1984

Peter Whelan has asserted his right under the Copyright, Designs and
Patents Act, 1988, to be identified as Author of this work.

British Library Cataloguing-in-Publication Data
A catalogue record for this book is available from the British Library.

ISBN: PB: 978-1-4081-3710-9
ePDF: 978-1-4081-3711-6
epub: 978-1-4081-3712-3

Library of Congress Cataloging-in-Publication Data
A catalog record for this book is available from the Library of Congress.

Typeset by Mark Heslington, Scarborough, North Yorkshire
Printed and bound in India

Contents

Peter Whelan: A Chronology   vii

Introduction   ix

THE ACCRINGTON PALS   1

Questions and Activities   107

Peter Whelan: A Chronology

Born: 3 October 1931, Newcastle-under-Lyme, Staffordshire

Plays
1970	*Lakota* (with Don Kincaid)
1975	*Double Edge* (with Leslie Darbon)
1978	*Captain Swing*
1981	*The Accrington Pals.* First performed 10 April 1981 by the Royal Shakespeare Company at the Warehouse, London, directed by Bill Alexander
1982	*Clay*
1983	*A Cold Wind Blowing Up* (with Leslie Darbon)
1986	*World's Apart,* adapted from a work by Jose Triana
1991	*The Bright and Bold Design*
1992	*The School of Night*
1993	*Shakespeare Country*
1995	*The Tinder Box* (adapted from Hans Christian Andersen)
1996	*Divine Right*
1997	*Overture*
1998	*The Herbal Bed*
1999	*Nativity*
2001	*A Russian in the Woods*
2004	*The Earthly Paradise*

Major professional productions of *The Accrington Pals:*
1982	Bolton Octagon
1983	Library Theatre, Manchester
1984	Hudson Guild Theater, New York
1986	Oldham Coliseum Theatre
1988	Perth Theatre
1990	New Vic, Newcastle-under-Lyme
2002	Chichester Festival Theatre

| 2003 | West Yorkshire Playhouse |
| 2005 | The Duke's, Lancaster |

In addition to these, *The Accrington Pals* has had numerous amateur and student productions throughout the UK.

Introduction

Synopsis

Act One, Scene One

Early on a cold winter morning in 1914 **Tom Hackford** is setting up the greengrocer's stall he helps **May Hassal** to run. He has a hangover as a result of the previous night's celebrations for today's departure of The Accrington Pals regiment for training in Caernarvon, North Wales. Tom has volunteered for the regiment and is wearing his army kit under his rain cape. May arrives, both angry with him and concerned for him. **Arthur Boggis**, also in uniform, enters; he is acting as knocker-up for the early-rising workers and expresses his Christian sentiments. As he leaves, his teenage son, **Reggie**, enters, trying to avoid his mother as he has stayed out all night at the Pals' send-off. **Ralph** (also in uniform) arrives with **Eva**, his girlfriend, who has left her job on a farm some distance away in the belief that she can take Tom's job as assistant to May on the stall and possibly the room in which he lodges with May. Tom has forgotten to mention any of this to May, but May spares Eva's embarrassment by immediately accepting her temporarily both as assistant and lodger. **Annie Boggis** comes looking for her son with the intention of hitting him in punishment – after several rather comic attempts she succeeds. **Sarah Harding** and **Bertha Treecott**, both mill-workers, arrive and witness this in amusement. There is a short blackout signifying a ten-minute gap in time as factory hooters and the 'clog chorus' (the noise of workers' wooden clogs on cobbles) are heard. May and Eva then discuss the area of Accrington; we see them warming to each other. Eva mentions that she's heard of May's attempt to get Tom's enrolment in the regiment reversed. May sends Eva off to put the kettle on while she packs up the stall. She pauses and is thinking of that attempt as **Company Sergeant Major Rivers** enters in shirt-sleeves and begins shaving. This is the beginning of the flashback which becomes Scene Two.

Scene Two

In discussion with CSM Rivers May reveals that Tom is her second cousin who came at a young age to live with her family after his parents died. Rivers says that it is not possible to release Tom from his commitment to the Pals, but assures May that he will keep a close, fatherly eye on him.

Scene Three

The flashback over, the scene returns to mid-morning of the day of the Pals' departure. Eva, Sarah and Bertha are joined by an excited Ralph who encourages Tom to finish a sketch of Eva which Ralph can take with him. At his request, she kisses it. Arthur arrives with his favourite pigeon, England's Glory, in a basket to take with him. He offers up a public prayer. May refuses to leave the stall to go to the station to see Tom and the Pals off. He remains behind and there is a tense scene in which she tries to give him money and he tries to kiss her. They struggle and he strides off, banging the money down on the stall and leaving May shaken.

Scene Four

Sarah and Eva are in May's kitchen three months later, discussing the censoring of the news of the war. The Pals have still not left England, but are being moved to Staffordshire. May arrives and surprises Sarah by being uncharacteristically friendly to her. After Sarah leaves May and Eva discuss Tom and Ralph, with May revealing some of her family history and Eva revealing that she has slept with Ralph. May is surprised but accepts it, saying that she is 'not a prude'. Eva goes off to bed, leaving May working on her accounts. There is a transition to the next scene, with Tom appearing on guard at the training camp before May leaves.

Scene Five

CSM Rivers arrives and checks on Tom. He asks after May and shares with Tom his idea of the comradeship which exists between soldiers. In another transition after Rivers leaves, Tom, now on leave, moves into May's kitchen.

Scene Six

Tom hears the sounds of Eva and Ralph making love upstairs. May, in nightdress and coat, joins him. She is disturbed by what Eva and Ralph are doing under her roof, but indicates her warmth of feeling to Eva. Tom expresses his belief in a society based on 'a free exchange of skills' but May dismisses him as a 'dreamer'. Tom takes her hand but she is unable to respond. He is angered and disappointed and she feels inhibited by their past.

Scene Seven

Arthur, in uniform, with the pigeon basket containing England's Glory beside him, reads out a letter to a friend back in Accrington. He gives the news that the Pals have moved to Ripon in Yorkshire and he comments on the sinfulness of the mill-owners in Accrington withholding proper payment from the workers. He justifies his decision as a man of religion to join the army to fight, suggesting that it is God's will.

Scene Eight

It is winter 1915 and a year has passed since the opening of the play. Eva, working on the stall, is joined by Sarah and Bertha, who is wearing a tram conductress's uniform. She talks about the sexist behaviour of the male tram workers and they also discuss the news censorship which is being imposed. Annie arrives looking for her son Reggie to punish him for yet another misdemeanour. She tells them the news that the Pals are going to be shipped to France in three weeks. They are all disturbed by this. After the others have left, May comments to Eva that she is wiser in her relationship with Ralph than she herself is in her relationship with Tom.

Scene Nine

Some weeks later Ralph is washing (naked) in a tin bath in May's kitchen while Tom sits repairing one of May's boots. Both are on leave. Eva enters and helps Ralph to wash. May arrives; she is embarrassed, but tolerant. She has bought a rabbit as a special treat for their dinner. When Ralph and Tom are out of the room May reveals that she is in mental torment about what to do about Tom. Tom enters carrying Reggie, who is streaming blood from his nose having been belted by his mother. Tom and May disagree about whether they should do anything about the situation, with May contending that they should not interfere. She compromises by promising Reggie a job and giving him threepence and an apple. Tom expresses his anger at the small-mindedness and political backwardness of the community. May sees this as an attack on her personally and tells him to get out. He does so. Ralph and Eva are shocked and insist that May go after him. She does so, hopelessly.

Scene Ten

At the stall May runs into CSM Rivers. He has just seen Tom heading for the Manchester train, presumably going to Salford where his aunt lives. Rivers speaks warmly of the quality of the men in the Pals, their sense of duty and service. May's response is: 'He wanted the Pals and he's got the Pals.' As she leaves Rivers, we hear a low rumble of guns and machine-gun fire.

Act Two, Scene One

Summer 1916. The scene opens with the sound which closed
Act One – distant machine guns. We see Ralph in one part of
the stage and Eva in another. He is addressing her, although
he knows she cannot hear him. He is ill and exhausted. He
reveals that the Pals have been in Egypt, but not seen real
action there, but now in France, he knows that 'the big push'
is coming soon. The light fades on him and intensifies on
Eva in May's kitchen. She is sewing the 'Britannia' costume
for her solo at a forthcoming concert for the war effort. May
enters and helps her, telling her that she has found a shop to
rent in another part of town, and invites Eva to move there
with her and be a partner in it. Eva questions her about her
intentions in relation to Tom, saying that she thinks May is
not being honest about her own feelings for him. The scene
finishes with May saying that Eva's comments have hurt her.
In the blackout at the end of the scene an artillery barrage is
heard.

Scene Two

Again in two separate areas of the stage we see Tom and
May; she is trying to do her accounts, he is reading out a
letter to her. He thanks her for gifts of food and promises to
send her sketches of the Pals and of herself.

Scene Three

May, Sarah, Bertha and Eva are drinking beer in May's
kitchen in celebration of what they believe will be the
approaching end of the war. They discuss men, including
Bertha's possible suitor whom she feels unable to accept as
he hasn't gone to war, having failed the medical. May, who is
slightly drunk, says that she finds the whole business of love
so 'bestial'. After she goes to bed, Sarah suggests to Eva that she
should leave May.

Scene Four

The first part of the scene shows the Pals (Tom, Ralph, Arthur and CSM Rivers) preparing to go 'over the top' at the Battle of the Somme. As they advance, the focus switches to Eva in her Britannia costume singing 'Oh Peaceful England' at the fundraising concert. After a minute she forgets a line and runs off angrily.

Scene Five

Sarah's back yard. Anne enters looking for Reggie to punish for teaching a dirty rhyme to younger children. She forces him to repeat it to Sarah, who has heard it all before. Bertha enters in excitement with a copy of the local paper, claiming imminent victory for the British forces. May and Eva join them to share the good news. During the scene, the injured and bloodied England's Glory (Arthur's pigeon) is spotted. Annie becomes hysterical and irrational, certain that Arthur has been killed. Eva takes the pigeon off to drown it.

Scene Six

The following day, alone in May's kitchen, Eva sits by the tin bath and imagines Ralph in it. May enters and starts talking business, but Eva is convinced that Ralph has been killed in the push and raises her hand to May, offended by her insistent refusal to accept what all the others believe about the war. May tells her that she should leave.

Scene Seven

At May's stall Reggie tells her of the distressed mental state of his mother, who is suffering from delusions. Bertha arrives, followed by Sarah who has heard the rumour that only seven of the almost 700 Pals have survived. Eva arrives to hear her say this. All except May go off to the Town Hall to demand the truth from the Mayor. May says she will find out about Tom in her own way. There follows a non-naturalistic sequence in which May finds herself in the trenches where she meets the dead CSM Rivers, who tells her almost a hundred Pals have survived and coaches her in the shooting of a rifle. As she fires it, the dead Tom appears as the target. Rivers maintains that Tom has died a hero, but May accuses him of dying as a slave, taken in by a delusion of comradeship. She reaches out her hands to Tom; he touches them, striking a sense of cold through her. Rivers orders him to take part in the parade of 'the glorious dead'. May retreats to her stall.

Scene Eight

May and Reggie are at the stall. Eva arrives with her suitcase; she is going to her sister's to help her and her father. May asks her to read a poem from the local paper about the fate of the Pals, their heroism and those who grieve for them. Eva is angered by its inadequacy to express her feelings. She leaves. May sits by the stall. We hear a bugle band play.

The Historical Context (One)

In his notes on the setting, Whelan says, *'The background is reality. The Accrington Pals' battalion of Kitchener's New Army was raised and destroyed as described in the play.'*

The Great War (as it was known at the time – only later did it become World War One) involved many nations, but for Britain it began with the declaration of war against Germany on 4 August 1914. The British army was relatively low on numbers and, at that time, conscription was not seen politically as an acceptable option. Within a few days of the declaration, Lord Horatio Kitchener, the newly appointed Secretary of State for War, issued an appeal for 100,000 volunteers. They had to be between nineteen and thirty, at least five feet three inches tall (1.6 metres) and with a chest measurement of at least thirty-four inches (eighty-six centimetres). They were known as 'Kitchener's New Army'.

The well-known poster of the walrus-moustached Lord Kitchener, pointing his finger directly at the viewer with the caption 'Your country needs YOU!', is remembered (and much imitated) now. It was suggested that men could be induced to sign up more readily if they were with groups of people they already knew and this led to the creation of 'Pals' regiments, based on particular towns or regions. At some recruiting centres queues were more than a mile long. Eventually almost 2.5 million men volunteered.

The Mayor of Accrington (who features as an off-stage character in the play) took the lead in the recruiting of the new battalion, which was raised within ten days. Although informally known as 'The Accrington Pals', the battalion's formal name was The 11th Battalion, The East Lancashire Regiment. At the time this was the structure of the army, going from the largest unit (the army itself) to the smallest unit (the section):

Army > Corps > Division > Brigade > Battalion > Company > Platoon > Section

A battalion consisted of about 1,000 men. About 250 men were from Accrington itself, with the remainder from surrounding areas. After training, the Accrington Pals joined the 94th Brigade of the British 31st Division and were sent to Egypt in early 1916 to defend the Suez Canal against the Ottoman Empire. (In Act Two Scene One, Ralph refers to himself as having been ready to fight 'Johnny Turk'.) They saw no serious action there, but were subsequently sent to France for 'the Big Push' (later known as the Battle of the Somme).

The intention of 'the Big Push' was to force the Germans to retreat from The Western Front, a line which they had held since 1914, and to weaken the German army by depleting their forces as well as affecting their morale. General Sir Douglas Haig's plan was to bombard the enemy with artillery for eight days so that the British infantry (foot soldiers) would meet little opposition. Over 1.7 million shells were fired in those eight days, but these made little impact on the deep dugouts and bomb-proof shelters of the Germans. When the bombardment finished, the Germans recognised this as an indication that the infantry attack was due and positioned their gunners accordingly. At 7.20 a.m. on 1 July 1916 the British forces began the advance over a twenty-five mile front. On this day the British army suffered 58,000 casualties, with a third of this number killed – making it the worst day in the history of the British army. This was the Accrington Pals' first day of real action. Of the 720 men in the battalion, 235 were killed and about 350 wounded within half an hour of 'going over the top', most mown down by German machine-gun fire as they walked towards the German trenches. Extraordinarily, some of the Pals managed to avoid the bullets and reached the enemy's trenches, but did not then survive. By the end of the day 584 were listed as killed, wounded or missing.

The play makes it clear that official published reports of battles in newspapers were intended to maintain morale at home rather than provide accurate information; these reports openly acknowledged that censorship prevented details being published. Letters from the front were also censored (or men self-censored them, knowing that information would be subject to censorship). The initial reports of the battle in *The Accrington Observer* which feature in Act Two Scene Five speak of the 'victorious troops' and the enemy being 'panic-stricken'. The off-stage incident in the play in which the local inhabitants go to the town hall demanding to know the truth from the Mayor of Accrington is historically true. It was he, of course, who had promoted the call for volunteers for the battalion.

The names of the dead are commemorated on the cenotaph which stands in Oak Hill Park, Accrington.

However, the play's main focus is on the lives of those who did not go into battle, especially on the women who were left behind. During the war women took on occupations which had previously been the sole preserve of men. With so many men on active service (and with so many failing to return or being wounded), there were severe shortages of labour in many industries. To fill this gap, women worked in factories and on the land, fulfilling traditional male roles. In Act One, Scene Eight, Bertha is seen in her tram conductress's uniform and there is discussion of women working in munitions factories. It is clear from Bertha's comments that the men resent their territory being invaded, but the nature of how women were seen in relation to work and the opportunities now open to them changed the face of society permanently. One result of this was that women over thirty were finally given the right to vote (suffrage) in 1918, as long as they were householders, were married to a householder or held a university degree. Universal suffrage (for all men and women over twenty-one) was not achieved until 1928.

The Historical Context (Two)

In an interview with the playwright Paul Wallis, Peter Whelan said:

> '*I've always said that I'm not a historian. I'm just using a story from history that happens to chime in with the things that I'm passionate about at the time. For me, therefore, this sort of piece shouldn't seem like a historical play, it should seem parallel with us, instead of it being in the past ... it should always be a play about today.*'

[Wallis, 1999]

Like all good plays about historical events, this play has a second historical context – that of the time when it was written and first produced (1979–81). In 1979, Margaret Thatcher, who had become the first woman leader of the Conservative Party in 1975, became Britain's first woman Prime Minister, having defeated Labour's James Callaghan in a General Election. She was keen to promote entrepreneurship. An entrepreneur is defined as a person who has possession of a new enterprise, venture or idea and assumes significant accountability for the inherent risks and the outcome – in other words, entrepreneurs are people who take individual responsibility for creating their own wealth through their own efforts. She was also keen to break the power of the trade unions, whose industrial action had done much to disrupt the running of the nation during the 1970s. In the play, May is very much in tune with this philosophy of 'self-help', behaving as an entrepreneur, taking responsibility for herself as an individual. Tom, on the other hand, represents the socialist view of a society based on 'the free exchange of skills' in which people band together for mutual support and do not exploit each other for individual gain. Whelan has commented that one of the central questions of life is, 'How much am I for myself and how much am I for other people?' and this debate was current in the Thatcher years. It is also central to the relationship between May and Tom.

The Play

Setting and Style
The set is extremely important to this play as it enables a fluid movement between geographically distant areas, a number of occasions when two locations are visible to the audience simultaneously and a non-naturalistic scene of a dreamlike – or nightmare-like – quality (the second part of Act Two, Scene Seven). Whelan notes that '*Minimal settings are intended, as there is a great deal of visual overlap between scenes, created by lighting changes.*' The two main areas are May's stall, covered by a tarpaulin when not in use, also providing the 'backdrop' to all the military scenes and the kitchen of May's small house. The set has to accommodate two other locations: the recruiting office in Act One and Sarah's backyard in Act Two.

Some scenes cross-fade into each other, suggesting connections between them – for example, Act One, Scene Four, which concludes with May thinking about Tom and the following scene which starts with Tom on guard duty at the training camp. At the end of this scene (Scene Five) Tom walks between areas on stage from the training camp to May's kitchen. Act Two Scene One begins with Ralph and

Eva both lit, one close to the front lines in France, the other in May's kitchen. The transition from Ralph's monologue to the scene between Eva and May is marked not just by the lighting change, but with the sound of machine guns giving way to the whirring of the sewing machine. There is a similar effect in Scene Four when both sound and lighting mark the transition from the battlefront to the concert in which Eva is singing. The device of having two separate areas visible to the audience simultaneously is repeated in Scene Two when we see both Tom and May. The boldest use of the staging comes in Scene Seven when May, standing against the stall's tarpaulin, encounters the dead CSM Rivers and Tom. At Rivers' instigation she fires a rifle at what turns out to be Tom.

The Accrington Pals is predominantly a realistic play, in that it deals with convincingly recognisable characters and behaviour, with language, costume, props and historical detail which are all credible as stage reality. One of its distinctive qualities is the ability to transcend this impression of reality by its use of setting, lighting and sound to produce powerful dramatic effects.

Structure

> *'There must be some kind of vision to inform it, something that hits you so hard and is so at one with your concerns, what you consider to be important ... you then need to bring an idea into collision with that vision to get the play going* ...The Accrington Pals *began with a vision.'*
>
> Peter Whelan, [Wallis, 1999]

The seed of the idea for *The Accrington Pals* was planted in Whelan's mind when he read Martin Middlebrook's book *The First Day on the Somme: 1 July 1916*. This provided the basic information about the history of the Pals, including both the false report that the Pals had been almost entirely wiped out and the subsequent the march on Accrington Town Hall, an off-stage event in the play. The 'vision' which kick-started the play came later. In conversation with the playwright Paul Wallis, Whelan spoke about this vision:

> *With* The Accrington Pals, *it was this vision of a trench in the First World War, and this woman in Edwardian dress going down the trench through hellfire, and she found a sort of alcove of the trench, and there was this sergeant major, and they were just looking at one another as the shells continued to explode. This is what I saw. I had no idea, in some ways, what it was about.*

[Wallis, 1999]

The vision eventually became part of Act Two Scene Seven, where May meets the dead CSM Rivers and Tom. The 'idea' which unlocked this vision was the relationship between May and Tom, with its personal and political dimensions (see the section on *Themes*). Of course, both the idea and the vision have to find expression in a narrative order and a sequence of scenes. Different playwrights work in different ways; some have to have a very clear idea of the structure before they can begin, but for others the structure emerges organically during the writing process. Whelan seems to be in the latter camp. This is part of the process of pursuing the 'vision' and marrying it with the 'idea'. '*...to me, embarking on a play is embarking on a mystery. I'll put it more strongly than that. I can only embark on a play if I'm absolutely convinced that I don't know what I'm doing.*' [Peter Whelan, quoted in Edgar, 1999, p.86] So, for Whelan, the writing is a process of discovery and finding the structure is part of that process. Nevertheless, Dominic Dromgoole has claimed that a number of Whelan's plays have a similar structure:

> '*In the first quarter or third of each play, he throws up a miasma of life ... digging out small, under-the-fingernails details ... characters fall onto the stage seemingly by accident; social and work information pours out seemingly at random; there are almost too many relationships to take in ... Then slowly, from this teeming mulch, patterns emerge. Certain relationships turn out to burn brighter than others;*

background influences start to exert a foreground pressure on
the characters; trivia starts to acquire weight.'
[Dromgoole, 2003, p.x]

Other than the fact that the play begins with the central relationship, that of May and Tom, this seems to be true of *The Accrington Pals*. Certainly, after the opening, the sense of teeming local life overtakes the stage as the various characters and their relationships are introduced. Gradually May becomes the centre of the play, as her relationships with Tom and Eva develop. We see the relationship between Tom and May against the background of the other 'pair' relationships in the play, but especially in comparison to the relationship between Ralph and Eva, whose physical and sexual ease with each other puts into context May's lack of ease and moral scruples. May envies Eva's instinctive qualities, which apply to both her relationship with Ralph and her 'political' instinct to march on the town hall. She cannot find these – or denies them – within herself, however. In the structure of the play we see points at which May increasingly isolates herself from those around her. At points we see her on the verge of a breakthrough – when she welcomes Sarah's visit in Act One Scene Four and embraces Tom in Act One Scene Six – but we see her order both Tom (Act One Scene Six) and Eva (Act Two Scene Six) from her house. An extraordinary sequence in Act Two Scene Seven sees her shooting the already dead Tom in her imagination – a symbolic act, which reflects her physical rejection of him (*'I should have loved you'*, she says to him). She seeks his condemnation to expiate her own guilt about the thought which she now reveals: *'I sat there ... and I thought it would be better if you didn't come back.'* It is as though she preferred the humdrum and safe quality of her life to the emotional turmoil of an intense relationship. The final scene with Eva (and Reggie) suggests that she will accommodate herself to this reduced life and carry on. This reflects Whelan's view that, in some sense, all plays are about survival.

Whelan has spoken about his interest (certainly at the time he was writing the play) in applying film techniques to the theatre; the setting is deliberately intended to enable this. So, in Scene Two we have a flashback to the scene between May and Rivers in which she tries, without success, to get him to release Tom from the army for which he has volunteered. Act One Scene Four cross-fades or 'dissolves' from May's kitchen to Tom's guard post in the following scene; at the end of that scene we 'track' Tom as he moves between the guard post and May's kitchen. In the second act, there are some uses of what is effectively a 'split-screen' technique: in Scene One we see Ralph and Eva in separate locations; in Scene Two the effect is repeated with May and Tom. The technique in Act Two Scene Seven by which reality fades into dream or imagination is very familiar to us from film. This fluidity enables Whelan to develop a 'dialectic' structure in which scenes are perceived in relation or counterpoint to each other.

Language

> 'You need to pay some attention to the language of the time, you have to use it to some extent, but mainly the language of our time ... I try not to be too anachronistic, but to get a melding between modern language and the language of the time, with a touch of the style of the period ...'
>
> Peter Whelan [Wallis, 1999]

Just as he writes not a play about history, but a play which raids history for a subject relevant to a modern audience, so Whelan 'raids' language for a sense of authenticity, while treating as his priority the necessity for the play to be immediately accessible to a modern audience. All the characters except CSM Rivers and Tom (who originally came from nearby Salford) are local to the Accrington area. Historically, it is likely that they would have had heavy local accents, but there is little attempt to present this in the play. Individual productions, notably one in Oswaldtwistle, very close to Accrington in Lancashire, have (with the playwright's permission) modified the language to reflect a stronger dialect – one, of course, which would still be recognisable to a modern local audience.

Some of the vocabulary of the play is intentionally and recognisably old-fashioned, although many of the words maintained their currency for a long time after the historical setting of the play, well into the 1950s and sometimes beyond. May accuses Tom of being a *'dolly daydream'* and recalls that Ralph has called her a *'tartar'*. She refers to *'the backs down the entries where Ralph lives'* that is, the area outside the backs of houses down alleyways. Sarah accuses Bertha of being *'a racy little thing'* for raising her skirt to 12 inches above the ground, and later says *'She's got a masher!'*, referring to the asthmatic electrician who is romantically interested in her. In all of these examples (and this goes for every other example in the play) the meaning in context is perfectly clear to a modern audience.

There are also old-fashioned expressions, which almost amount to clichés, which are part of the shared speech of the community. Bertha says self-deprecatingly, *'Even my father says I'm better followed than faced'* (i.e. her back view is better than her front view). Ralph, in the heat of the trenches, says, *'It's like a bake oven this summer night. I'm in a muck sweat.'* Bertha claims that she feels *'neither use nor ornament'*, an expression which means that she feels useless in every way. These expressions create the sense both of period and of the shared working-class culture.

There is also a pleasure which a number of the characters take in swearing, conscious that they are courting the disapproval of some more staid members of the community. (May, when slightly drunk, refers to *'This mean, dirty foul-mouthed place.'*) Ralph, in the first scene, says, *'Shall Accrington and district be behind?* (In a quick aside to **Tom**) *Shall they arseholes!'* Annie, who accuses Reggie of making her swear by his infuriating behaviour in the first scene (*'Oh, you bugger!'*) later addresses Sarah as *'Miss Piss'*. Sarah later uses the expression *'eyes ... like piss-holes in the snow'* to describe the appearance of her father with a hangover. There is a sense of a vibrant working-class culture in which the rather daring use of 'forbidden' language feels like a spirited defiance of some dead-handed authority.

The character who habitually uses grammatical constructions which belong to the local dialect is the youngest – Reggie. His first line is, '*Was that me father?*' and later, speaking of his distraught mother, he says, '*Her started screaming again … Her wanted rug out of kitchen burnt.*' With few exceptions, the other characters construct their utterances in standard grammatical ways.

Individual characters are recognisable by their style of speech and their vocabulary as well as by what they say. Tom speaks in short sentences, sometimes as though uttering a series of short reflections to himself ('*She gets my allowance. Hardly spend a bean in camp. You don't need to. That's the great thing about the army. You don't need money. Everything's found.*'). Arthur borrows the rhetoric of the Methodist Chapel ('*…we are all of us on the threshold of the celestial city…*'), and CSM Rivers adopts a semi-poetic, rhythmic style of assertion to express his belief in the comradeship to be found in the army ('*No one can divide us from each other*'). Sarah's language is peppered with a healthy and energetic vulgarity: '*…and I shall have Bill back picking his nose and spitting in the fire and breaking wind fit to blow the ornaments off the whatnot.*'

While all the characters have their distinctive style of speech, the overall impression of the language of the play gives a clear reflection of the working-class culture of the period, often involving a robust assertion of the realities of everyday life. But there is little in that language which would require a footnote, because, as Whelan notes in the quotation at the beginning of this section, he is mainly interested in creating a language which, while conveying a clear sense of period and place, communicates directly to a modern audience.

Themes

The roles and relationships of men and women

Peter Whelan conceived the play as being about 'what happened to the women back home' during the Great War, so the women's experience occupies a central part in the play. Traditionally, women were seen by many at this time as being the home-makers and the raisers of families. For working women there was an accepted range of occupations – as, indeed, there was for men. May suggests in Act One Scene One that men occupy a privileged position in the households: '*And the girls like to pick up a bit extra to eat when they're out of the house, for they get little enough at home. All the titbits go to their fathers and the brothers get what's left.*' Bertha's account of her experiences as a tram conductress in Act One Scene Eight hints at a widespread resentment by men of their work roles being usurped (as they see it) by women as the war progresses and conscription becomes inevitable. But it is also Bertha who cannot reconcile herself to the prospect of a proposal of marriage from a man who hasn't gone to war – even though the reason is not lack of courage, but that his asthma has led to failing the army medical. The play presents a range of attitudes held by one gender about the other; this is evident in an examination of the main male–female relationships in the play.

We are aware of the relationships of four couples in the play. We never see Sarah's husband, Bill, in the play, but we hear about him from her and we learn of her attitude to him. She sees him mainly in sexual terms: she speculates about his lack of resistance to the wild Welsh women she imagines tempting him in the training camp in Caernarvon; she becomes sexually frustrated during his prolonged absence with the Pals: '*…Bill. He's a steam-hammer. If he missed me, he'd have the bedroom wall down! I used to get weary of being pulverised, but I wouldn't mind now.*' (Act Two, Scene Three). Ralph and Eva also have a sexual relationship; Tom and May (and, of course, the audience) overhear part of their lovemaking in Act One Scene Six and we observe their

intimate relationship when Ralph is naked in the tin bath
in Act One Scene Nine. But they are unmarried and sexual
relationships outside marriage were regarded as immoral by
many at this time. For Eva, the relationship is not merely her
way of escaping the loneliness of farm life, but a genuine and
generous love. May speaks of her *'giving herself'* to Ralph, in
a way which suggests that she would normally disapprove
of such a thing – but such is the straightforwardness of Eva's
attitude that it begins to expand May's horizons and to
incline her to think that she might sleep with Tom. Ralph
commissions the drawing of Eva from Tom and when she
kisses it before he takes it away even the hardbitten Sarah
sees it as a romantic gesture. But we learn later from Ralph
(in the 'letter' in Act Two Scene One) that he has *'slept with
whores'* while in the army. This may make him long all the
more for Eva, but she, on the other hand, idealises him and
remains loyal to him. It appears that Annie has married
Arthur Boggis to avoid the stigma of being an unmarried
mother – but the child (Reggie) is not his (Act Two Scene
Six). Although she criticises Arthur (for example, for his
failure to reprimand Reggie), the extremity of her distress
on hearing the news of his death is shocking (*'I shall eat
stones, I shall eat stones…'* – Act Two, Scene Six). But none
of these relationships appears entirely balanced and equal.
The relationship of May and Tom is complicated by their
family history; Tom has been taken into May's family at a
young age after his parents died and, despite the ten-year
age-gap between them (he is nineteen, she about twenty-
nine), they have a background of shared experiences, like
going to see performances of Shakespeare's plays with her
drunken father. It is clear that there is a great deal of love
between them and both would like a love relationship, but
they are also themselves obstacles to that relationship. Their
attitudes to society and money differ radically (see below); he
is a progressive socialist believing in *'the free exchange of skills'*,
while she is a relentless self-helper, putting into practice her
belief that people have to make their own way, if necessary
at the expense of others, to succeed. In a key moment at the

end of Act One Scene Three when May and Tom struggle silently as he tries to embrace her, he comments angrily on the fact that she will give him money (she has tried to give him four pounds to take with him, a significant sum at that time), with the implication that she cannot give him the love he wants.

The political dimension
Gender politics, as indicated above, play a significant part in the play. In Act One Scene Eight Sarah, Bertha and Eva are discussing the attitude of the men to the women who are, for the first time, taking on traditional male working roles. Bertha says that the men claim that the women will 'want to be drivers next'. Sarah's response is an energetic (and entertaining) assertion of women's claims to equality:

Sarah   And why shouldn't you? If there's one thing that narks the men about this war it's the way it shows them up for creating such mysteries round things. My God! Providing both your eyes point forwards and your arms aren't stuck on back to front, anyone can drive a tram! Especially with their skirt twelve inches off the ground.

In the same scene Sarah points out the fact that it isn't only the men who are facing death and injury:

Sarah   What about the munitions girls ... the girls in Gretna Green that got blown to bits that they tried to hush up? And getting canary through working with TNT so you're coughing yellow cud the rest of your life?

('*Canary*' refers to a type of lung disease.)
    It is the women who, at Eva's instigation, march on the town hall and demand to know the truth about the Pals from the Mayor. Their direct action leads to the discovery of the distressing information about the terrible fate of the Pals. There is the sense of the women as a growing and positive force in society, increasingly aware of and prepared to assert their rights.

Dominic Dromgoole has pointed out that 'running through Whelan's plays there is ... a strong impression of the malignity of authority'. In *The Accrington Pals* an element of that is the traditional authority of the now beleaguered males defending their established roles. But we see it also in the Mayor, forced eventually (offstage) to tell the truth, in the voice of the press, acting as a tool of the Government not merely in censoring information, but in promulgating optimistic and inaccurate views of the war. We are also aware of the men of Accrington having been betrayed to their deaths by the authority of inept military leaders – 'lions led by donkeys' is the striking phrase which was applied to the troops a little later.

But the central political issue in the play is bound up with its central relationship – that of May and Tom. It is one of the factors that finally keeps them apart. The difference in their views has been referred to in the section on Historical Context (Two) above. May believes in the necessity of self-help, the importance of achieving independent economic survival through independent effort and entrepreneurship; she works hard to better herself and to develop and extend her business – and sees pricing up scarce items for those who can afford it as fair game. As she herself points out, the war is kind to her:

May   I never believed the war would make a difference like this. There's money around ... and there's shops that fell empty in the hard times you could have for really low rents. (Act One Scene Four)

Critics have spotted in her similarities to Brecht's Mother Courage, who makes her living from trading during war – but who loses all her children to it. Tom, younger and more idealistic, believes in a society in which trade (and money) will be unnecessary, where there will be a *'free exchange of skills'* – meaning that individuals will support each other by pooling their skills in a fair and equitable way. His experience in the army encourages him to see it as a model for this kind of society; soldiers support each other in a comradely spirit in this way, without the need for payment. Unsurprisingly, May thinks him naïve and a dreamer – a word she applies to him in the first scene. She uses it again in Act One Scene Six when Tom is explaining to her how the army has made him see the idea of the 'free exchange of skills' more clearly. But the contrast in their attitudes towards society goes deeper than this. In the second major flashpoint between them (the first occurs at the end of Act One Scene Three when they struggle silently as he tries to embrace her before leaving with the Pals) we see how Tom cannot accept the traditional entrenched attitudes of the local society. In Act One Scene Nine, Tom carries the young Reggie into May's kitchen. Reggie has been hit with a belt and is bleeding profusely from a wound near his nose, caused by the metal buckle. After the wound has been treated, Tom wants Reggie to stay there and rest up. May insists that he go back, as she sees keeping him there as 'interfering' in someone else's business. Tom bursts out in anger at the small-minded attitudes of the society:

Tom   They're stuck! Stuck! That's why everything's cockeyed. Stuck in their own little worlds. They can't see further than what they know. Mentally stuck. It's got that they think they'll go under for stepping beyond their own backyard.

May believes that he is referring to her and her attitudes and tells him to '*Get out of my sight*'. He goes and it is a striking feature of the play that they never see each other again – until the 'vision' sequence in Act Two Scene Seven, after his death.

Dromgoole says about Whelan's plays that '*the forces of history are felt, but only discreetly displayed*'. Here, the political debate is so integrated with the personal relationship that it becomes part of the whole.

Characters

Like many playwrights, Whelan draws on people he knows (or knows of) to provide characteristics for characters he creates in his plays. The character of May is based on an aunt whom he never met, but who occupied a place in family legend. Others are sometimes based on family members he does know. The result is that his characters have both solidity and credibility. The offstage life is often as significant as that onstage and we get our impression of the world of Accrington from what characters tell us. Sometimes this is reported, as in Sarah's comments about her husband, Bill, and her views about '*the posh lot, up Peel Park way*' to whom May sells her produce secretly. We sense Jack Burndred's character in the letter which Arthur writes to him (and he is mentioned again later in the play). We are aware of the march on the Town Hall and the attitude of the Mayor. Sometimes the sound effects of the '*clog chorus*' and the sewing machines create a sense of the society amidst which the play is set.

May is about twenty-nine (ten years older than Tom). Tom is her second cousin who has been taken in by May's father after his parents died. Thus they have been raised together. Although there is clearly a strong attraction between them, their differences, as seen by May, keep them apart (see section on *Themes*). After working in the mill, she has created an independent life for herself with her greengrocery stall, no doubt reacting against the incompetence of her father in business matters. Her independent spirit frequently keeps her aloof from others and she despises going along with 'the herd'. Inexperienced sexually and romantically, she struggles to give spoken and physical expression to her love for Tom, and ultimately feels that she has 'killed' their relationship by this apparent coldness. With Eva, she finds a confidante and envies her natural, intuitive ability to be in touch with her feelings and to express them easily. Eventually, however, she finds it impossible to accommodate the differences between them, and dismisses her from her life.

Eva is about nineteen and at the start of the play has come from nearby Clayton-le-Moors on the strength of what she believes is an arrangement to take over both Tom's work on the stall and the room where he lodges with May. She has been working on a farm, but later obtains a job at the mill while continuing to help on the stall. She has been having a relationship with Ralph, which she later tells May is sexual. She is naturally self-possessed and open, qualities which May admires and envies. She sees clearly what May needs to do in her relationship with Tom and ultimately cannot understand May's perverseness in asserting her independence to her own disadvantage. Distressed by Ralph's death and May's attitude, she eventually raises her hand to strike her, effectively signalling the end of their relationship. In the final scene we learn that she is going to live with her sister to support their 'incapable' father.

Sarah is a married mill-worker in her mid-twenties. We never see her husband, Bill, but we are given a vivid impression of a bullish, highly-sexed man from Sarah's descriptions. She is earthy and vulgar and very aware of the position which women hold in the society of the day in contrast to the men. She doesn't hide her sexual nature, saying how the sight of a sailor on leave has made her go '*ting-a-ling*' and how she fancies the '*tall bronzed Australians and Canadians*'. She also has a romantic side – she comments that her '*knees have turned to water*' when Eva kisses the sketch which Tom has done for Ralph. She is a clear contrast in this respect to the repressed May.

Bertha is a mill-girl of eighteen at the start of the play. She later becomes a tram conductress, as women begin to occupy traditional male roles. In contrast to her friend Sarah, she is naive and rather gullible – she accepts as gospel the story of the two Germans hiding in a coffin with a machine gun.

She seems to live by simple moral codes, as exemplified
by her inability to accept the advances of the asthmatic
electrician – '*I couldn't love a man who stayed at home*'. She is
sometimes apparently not intelligent enough to spot Sarah's
sarcasm to her. She provides a further contrast to May, who
is inexperienced but not naive, and to Sarah, as she lacks her
sharpness and perception.

Annie is a housewife in her late thirties, married to Arthur
Boggis. Their child is Reggie – we regularly see her
trying to catch and physically punish him for his various
misdemeanours. While this is initially comic, the seriousness
of the wound inflicted on him in Act One Scene Nine by
the belt buckle is not amusing. Annie has married the
very religious Arthur after having had Reggie by another
man. She seems to have been forced into living a life which
goes against her nature, unsupported in her handling
of Reggie by Arthur and forced to adopt his moralising
attitudes publicly. While she can be a harridan (and the
butt of humour for characters like Ralph and Sarah) we get
glimpses of the much warmer, freer person she might have
become – for example when she is shocked into laughter by
Sarah's remark about the fact that Jesus had no children –
'*None that they mention in the Bible, anyway.*' The scene in which
she breaks down mentally after realising that Arthur has
died is shocking in its impact.

Tom is nineteen and an apprenticed lithographer, having
had training at art school. Brought up in Salford, his parents
died when he was young. He has socialist and progressive
views in contrast to the traditional and conservative views of
May. He is impulsive and in some ways immature. Rather
than try to discuss matters with May in their argument after
caring for Reggie's wound, he finds it easier to go away on
the train to Salford. He believes that he finds in the army
an example of his desired society, based on '*the free exchange
of skills*'. The 'Tom' that we see in the penultimate scene is a

dead demonic character, with only a small vestige of the Tom we have known in the play.

Ralph is also nineteen, a clerk, keen to escape the drudgery of his work by enlisting. He is a more 'laddish' character than Tom, more outgoing and cheeky. He makes fun of Annie Boggis and sneaks upstairs to make love to Eva in May's house. In the 'letter' he reads to Eva in Act Two, Scene One, he speaks of the whores he has slept with, although he sits on a doorstep and cries for Eva after one of these episodes. He cannot understand the subtleties of Tom and May's relationship ('*It's put me in a right fog*'). His uncomplicated laddishness contrasts with Tom's gentleness and sensitivity. He goes to his death at the Somme with a desperate, fearful courage.

Arthur (married to Annie) is defined by his religion (he is a Primitive Methodist). He insists on leading everyone in prayer in the street before the Pals depart. His marriage with Annie seems ill-matched – but he is devoted to his pigeons, especially the ironically named 'England's Glory' which returns maimed and dying to Accrington from the Somme. He believes that God will see the wickedness of the mill-owners in withholding proper pay from the workers and he sees the war as a second Flood – a punishment from God; this, to him, justifies his taking up arms. Rivers, in the penultimate scene, refers to him in the battle as 'refusing God', suggesting that his faith, at the last, was broken.

Reggie is fourteen or fifteen, and generally in trouble with his mother for a variety of adolescent misdemeanours – staying out all night, playing 'knock down ginger' (tying doorknockers together) or teaching dirty rhymes to younger children. One of his functions in the play is to provide a catalyst for the argument between Tom and May (Act One Scene Nine). By the end of the play he is helping May on the stall – and apparently on the way to becoming a useful citizen.

Company Sergeant Major Rivers is the most shadowy character in the play – and the only true 'outsider'. He is an experienced professional soldier – he speaks of being in the Sudanese desert, which implies that he has served in the wars there at some time between 1881 and 1898. May finds herself shy in his presence. He has a kind of inscrutability which differentiates his character from any other in the play. Whelan has said that there is a symbolic significance in the choice of his name, relating to the classical 'rivers of death', the Styx, Acheron and Lethe. He becomes identified with Charon, who ferries dead souls across the river to the underworld. In the penultimate scene we see him assembling the army of the dead to march, presumably into the afterlife – '*Move yourselves, you glorious dead*'.

John Davey, 2010

Bibliography

Dromgoole, D. (ed.), *The Full Room* (London: Methuen, 2002)

Dromgoole, D., Introduction to *Peter Whelan: Plays 1* (London: Methuen, 2003)

Edgar, D. (ed.), *State of Play: Playwrights on Playwriting* (London: Faber & Faber, 1999)

Ellis, S., 'I look at the spaces between people', *Guardian*, 23 November 2004

Middlebrook, M., *The First Day on the Somme: 1 July 1916* (London: Penguin, 2006)

Nightingale, B., '1916 and all that', *Times*, 25 January 2002

Sunderland, Charles Spencer, Earl of, 'Flesh and blood in a time of war', *Daily Telegraph*, 25 Jan, 2002

Taylor, P., 'Theatre: Life on the home front', *Independent*, 24 January 2002

Wallis, P., Unpublished interview with Peter Whelan (1999)

Whelan, P., *Peter Whelan: Plays 1* (London: Methuen, 2003)

The Accrington Pals

To Tom

Author's Preface

As a child I was fascinated by a fuzzy snapshot of my mother taken in the First World War. It was the time she volunteered as a female lumberjack ... or was it 'lady forester'? I could hardly credit it. A less likely feller of trees than my mother I couldn't imagine, yet there she was, leaning in a very posed, dewy-eyed Edwardian fashion on the upturned handle of a full-blooded woodsman's axe, somewhere in the Home Counties ... a million miles from the Salford street she grew up in (an exact twin of *Coronation Street,* now bulldozed away for ever).

I suppose what I couldn't believe was that my mother as I knew her then ... stout, middle-aged and living entirely for her family ... had ever experienced such release. Doors had once been opened and then slammed shut, as they had been for millions of young women in that war. And through the doors they had glimpsed tantalising freedom as well as unimaginable horrors.

So I think I'd always wanted to write something about working-class women in the Great War. Then, maybe nine or ten years ago, I read Martin Middlebrook's *The First Day on the Somme,* a pulverising account of Britain's awakening to machine-age violence.

One short paragraph stayed in my mind. It concerned the town of Accrington, Lancashire which had raised its own battalion, 'The Accrington Pals', for Kitchener's New Army. After the Somme battle, Middlebrook tells us how the townspeople, driven desperate by rumours of disaster and angered by ludicrously optimistic reports in the press, surrounded the Mayor's house to demand the truth.

For me this was like looking through a pinhole into the past and finding a whole vista of humanity revealed in a very unexpected way. These mothers, wives, daughters and lovers of the Pals didn't knuckle under sheepishly to authority in the way I had supposed. They realised perfectly well that there was an 'us and them' situation with regard to war information. Soldiers and sailors on leave contradicted the official handouts. Those women resented government secrecy then as we do today and suspected, as we do, that much of it was a cover-up for blundering at the top.

Now I had the background for a play but not the foreground. That came to me two years ago while sitting in The Other Place during breaks in rehearsals of *Captain Swing*. There were a lot of sounds of clogs on bare boards in that play and the sounds took me back to a Lowry-like picture of Salford as I dimly recalled it from childhood, when visiting my uncles and aunts.

I began to evolve the story of a clash-cum-love relationship between a strong-minded, rugged individualist woman and a dreamy, Utopian idealist young man. Such a relationship was very much in keeping with those early years of the century when there were two clear ways that working people could see of improving their lot. One was the individualistic route – get yourself a little corner shop, etc. The other was through collectivism and trade unionism. And since my family at that time contained both shopkeepers and 'dreamy' socialists, it held a vivid basic attraction for me. I was now dealing not with history but with the edge of living memory. Details of my family folklore came to me in a rush.

One evening at a crowded pub in Stratford I grabbed the unsuspecting parents of one of the actors and poured out the whole story to them with frequent stops for adjustments and digressions. I hope I bought them a drink afterwards. So background and foreground had now come together in that explosive way that sustains a writer through the actual process of putting the play down on paper.

In choosing a self-confessed individualist for my main character, I hope I am being conscious, without being artificially conscious, of contemporary parallels. It seems like the wheel turning full circle that the Samuel Smiles self-help mentality is back in the political arena.

Older working-class generations may remember how the rows between paddle-your-own-canoe individualists and socialist-inclined trade unionists split families down the middle. Now the wedge is being driven in again. And maybe it's one of the basic contradictions that split personalities, let alone families. How much am I for others? How much am I for myself? Twenty years ago I might have said that the reconciliation of this contradiction was the answer to the Socratic question: how shall we live? But today it takes on a global urgency as we face the question: how shall we survive?

We are all crossing no-man's-land now.

Peter Whelan
1982

Thirty Years On . . .

The very alert, grey-haired man shaking my hand was dressed in the uniform of a Chelsea Pensioner and was introduced to me as one of the original Pals. We were at the Warehouse Theatre (now the Donmar) back in 1981 for the premiere of Bill Alexander's richly observed RSC production. I think and hope the old soldier enjoyed it . . . and the celebratory drinks afterwards, at the pub on the corner.

The point is that there were plenty of people around in those days who had lived through, or fought in, the First World War . . . so for me it remained very much a part of my contemporary world. But this year, with the last battlefield survivors reportedly gone, the war is quietly slipping into history . . . yet a history that hangs over our past like a blood-red sun.

Tragically, in the thirty years since writing the play there's been no shortage of fresh wars. We've fought four (or five) of them in that short space of time. The Kaiser's Prussian menace may be a sepia memory, but red-tabbed British regimentalism marches on . . . a pathetic mini-presence on the global stage.

What else has, or hasn't, changed? In the realm of sexual politics – I have May Hassal, talking to Eva about her cotton mill job: 'They don't pay you the same as they pay a man, do they?' she says. This may have been a simmering injustice in the world of 1916 but, surely, by the 1980s we already had the Equal Pay Act, didn't we? And yet here we are thirty years later with women still trailing . . . and research by the Chartered Management Institute showing that for women managers (to give but one example) it's going to take fifty-seven years for equal pay to become reality!

As for Tom Hackford, would he have believed that governments of millionaires would still be possible nearly a century after his time? The Cameron coalition of today would certainly make him think that 'those who lord it over here' were back in power ... and Ralph would see the cutting of jobs in the public services as 'nothing but a bloody lockout'.

But what never changes for me with the years is the emotional pull of family connections in the play. I secretly poached on my parents' territory . . . I shamelessly raided memories of their and my uncles' and aunts' young generation. I invaded that mysterious region of their intimate relationships. Well, the passage of three decades has softened the writer's guilt at such plundering. Today, reading this welcome new edition (thank you, Methuen) or being at a new performance, I still catch an echo of far-off voices and sense again how their life and mine are one.

P.S. I learned a few months ago that no record of the Boys' Brigade in Accrington in 1914 could be found. In which case we'll have to assume a neighbouring community had a company available. Boys' Brigade bands were one of my earliest musical experiences ... they just have to be there!

Peter Whelan
August 2010

The Accrington Pals was first performed by the Royal Shakespeare Company at the Warehouse, London, on 10 April 1981. The cast was as follows:

Tom	Nicholas Gecks
May	Janet Dale
Arthur	Andrew Jarvis
Reggie	Vincent Hall
Ralph	Peter Chelsom
Eva	Trudie Styler
Annie	Brenda Fricker
Sarah	Sharon Bower
Bertha	Hilary Townley
CSM Rivers	Bob Peck

Directed by Bill Alexander
Designed by Kit Surrey
Lighting by Michael Calf
Sound by John A. Leonard
Music arranged by Peter Washtell

Characters

May, *a stallholder, late twenties or older*
Tom, *an apprentice, nineteen*
Ralph, *a clerk, nineteen or so*
Eva, *a mill girl, the same age as Ralph*
Sarah, *a married mill worker, mid-twenties*
Bertha, *a mill girl, eighteen*
Annie, *a housewife, late thirties*
Arthur, *her husband, of similar age*
Reggie, *her son, fourteen/fifteen*
CSM Rivers, *a regular soldier, thirties/forties*

Setting

Two main stage areas: May's street-corner greengrocery stall in Accrington and the kitchen of her two-up two-down terraced house nearby.

The stall, when closed, serves as a backdrop to the military scenes at camp in England, or on the Western front.

The variations on this general scheme are the recruiting office in Act One and Sarah's backyard in Act Two.

Minimal settings are intended, as there is a great deal of visual overlap between scenes, created by lighting changes.

The action takes place between autumn 1914 and July 1916. The background is reality. 'The Accrington Pals' battalion of Kitchener's New Army was raised and destroyed as described in the play. Otherwise all the characters in the play, and the events of their lives, are entirely fictitious.

Note on the music

'My Drink is Water Bright' (Act One, Scene One) used a hymn tune called 'Merry Dick', but it goes quite well to 'Old Soldiers Never Die'.

'Boys Brigade March'

Act One

Scene One

The market stall, closed up; a winter morning.

Tom Hackford *pulls on a hand cart of greengroceries. He unties the stall covers, lights the lamp and begins to transfer the produce to the stall. He wears a rain cape under which we can see his army trousers, puttees and army boots.*

May Hassal *enters, a shawl over her head, the iron scales in one hand, an enamel jug of tea in the other. She has a grudge against him and he knows it.*

May   So. You got up.

Tom   As per.

May   You look like a corpse.

Tom   It's cold enough.

May   I wasn't talking about the cold. Shove those baskets back.

As he does so she places the scales on the stall.

Tom   It's laying off a bit. Was raining stair rods at quarter to five.

May   I saw.

Tom   Oh?

May   I could see through the window. I was awake listening for you getting out in case you weren't capable.

Tom   I'm all right.

He begins to flick and stamp his boot.

May   You'll injure your brains.

Tom   Dratted things let water in.

May   They weren't issued for working.

Tom   They'll have to stand up to worse than this on manoeuvres.

May (*pouring tea into mugs*)   That's a word you love isn't it?

Tom   What?

May   Manoeuvres. (*She hands him a mug.*) Stir that or you won't taste the sugar.

Tom   When it comes down to doing anything properly, they've got no idea. Someone decides that because a boot's for marching then it must have a thick sole. They don't think about the weight of the sole pulling down on the uppers. They don't consider the nature of the material. If the sole was three-quarters as thick ... or even half ... so it could flex as you marched it would actually wear longer. But if you said that they wouldn't understand. It's the same with the way they run everything. They're boneheads. They don't comprehend.

May   We'll have a ha'penny on carrots.

Tom *gives a disapproving look.*

May   A ha'penny. I don't make the shortages. They're a penny a pound on at the Co-op.

Tom *takes the blackboard and rechalks the price.* **May** *regards him for a while.*

May   You think I'm going to say nothing don't you?

Tom   About what?

May   When it comes down to it ... at the end ... you're on your own. Oh Tom, whatever did you think you were doing last night?

Tom   How d'you mean?

May   You and Ralph and the rest, making all that noise outside the house at gone midnight.

Tom We thought you'd still be up.

May What's the difference whether I was up or down? You woke every family in the street.

Tom Just a bit of a send-off. Some of them were with us.

May Who were?

Tom Neighbours.

May Then I'm even more ashamed. You've never seen me cry have you?

Tom *shakes his head.*

May Well, I came close to it last night.

Tom You could have come along.

May I wouldn't waste my existence. Stinking pipes, stale beer and smutty songs. No sir, not me. You can think it's a celebration, marching off to camp. Well march away! After what I heard you shout last night I'm glad to see you go.

Tom What?

May I heard you from the bedroom. 'I'm free of her!' I heard you distinctly, top of your voice. 'I'm free of her!' It was you. My father put a roof over your head when you came here from Salford. We gave you work so you'd have pocket money. And when he died I could have said: I'm sorry Tom, you'll have to leave. We can't share the same house. But I didn't. I could see you couldn't afford to. I let you stay on and I made it clear in every way you were under no obligation. And now I see you've treated it as some form of bondage. 'I'm free of her!'

Tom I didn't say that.

May You did. Shouted it so everyone could hear. You slighted me.

Tom I didn't say 'free of *her*'. I said 'free of *here*'.

May   Oh don't demean yourself.

Tom   Free of here ... of this place ... of this town.

May   Of this town?

Tom   That's what I meant.

May   But you've always preferred Accrington to Salford.

Tom   Aye. But that's not saying much is it?

May   You twister! (*Laughs.*) You almighty twister!

Tom   There's no twisting in it.

May   You may be a dreamer. You may go on about improving the mind and your world's famous thinkers ... but you're a twister. I won't say another word. March away! If you can. I heard you fall down three times on the stairs last night.

Tom   I'll have to sign the pledge again.

May   You? They'll have drummed you out of the Band of Hope for good and all!

Tom (*sings*)   'My drink is water bright ... water bright ... water bright.'

May   Where's the plums?

Tom   Oh ... aye ... they hadn't got none.

May   They had.

Tom   They hadn't. The waggoner's gone to France in the artillery. The old man that's taken over does it all at a snail's pace apparently ... he hadn't shown up.

May   They hide them! If there's a shortage they'll tell you all sorts! You have to ferret and burrow and not take 'no'. All the result of that is they'll have plums on the market stalls and we'll have none in Waterloo Street and you know how the girls like a plum on their way to work. But you're out of it aren't you? Dreamer!

Tom   What's it to do with dreaming?

May   Oh you're so obstinate and you know perfectly well.
Dreaming is not making your own decisions but letting
others make them for you. There are some kinds of men that
are forever making themselves prey for others ... falling in ...
getting swept along. And they're so overjoyed when they're
welcomed in by their new cronies ... 'Young Tom! Move
along for young Tom ... what'll you drink Tom?' I don't
want to see you like that, throwing all away for a little bit of
buttering up. Cos all they want to see is you failing. They love
failure. Delight in it. They see someone like you who has the
ability to get on and they're just waiting to see you stumble,
slip back and be as they are. In the end it's you ... yourself.
We don't create the rules of life. They're there.

Tom   Then it depends which way you read them.

A silence.

*Presently we hear the knocker-up approaching, tapping on the
windows with a pole to wake the mill girls.*

Arthur (*off*)   Rise and shine Elsie James ... quarter to six.

Arthur Boggis *enters. He is in uniform with a gas cape. He taps at
a window.*

Arthur   Are you in there Mrs Bloor and Brenda? Quarter
to six. Rise and shine.

May   What are you doing, knocking up, Arthur?

Arthur   Morning May ... Tom. Jack's got the sciatica and as
I was to be up early for the great day I said I'd do this end of
the street while his son does the other.

May   So it's you that's ruined the weather.

Arthur   It's God's weather.

May   Ah, but does He get wet in it?

Arthur   A question I've never asked.

Tom `Well look! It's clearing up. Is that a sign?

Arthur   It can be if you want it to be. But why look for signs when the true destination is always before you? We are all of us on the threshold of the celestial city if we have hearts to see with. (*He taps another window.*) Rise and shine Mary ... (*He pauses looking at his watch.*) Thirteen minutes to six.

He goes.

May   Pull the pears to the front seeing there's no plums ...

Reggie Boggis *enters furtively.*

May   What are you up to Reggie?

Reggie   Was that me father?

May   You know it was.

Reggie   Has Mother been out?

May   Any minute. Why?

Reggie   Haven't been home.

Tom   All night?

May   She'll paddle you!

Reggie   I know.

Tom   Make yourself scarce.

May   Don't interfere.

Reggie   I was at the Pals sing-song wasn't I Mr Hackford?

May *gives* **Tom** *a look.*

Tom   I didn't see him.

May   Wait round the corner. I don't want her paddling you here.

As **Reggie** *goes he almost collides with* **Ralph** *who is in uniform and carrying a suitcase.*

Ralph   Go get your bugle Reggie! Chorley's up and
marching. Blackburn's forming fours! (*Aside to* **Tom**.) What
she say? Is it all right?

Before **Tom** *can answer* **May** *rounds on* **Ralph**.

May   You! Bawling and caterwauling last night spoiling
people's sleep.

Ralph   England shake off your downy slumbers. Men of
Lancashire all parts of the Empire are responding nobly to
the call. Shall Accrington and district be behind? (*In a quick
aside to* **Tom**.) Shall they arseholes!

Eva Mason *has entered, carrying her belongings in an old carpet
bag. She stands apart shyly.* **Ralph** *introduces her as though* **May**
should know her. **Tom** *looks guilty.*

Ralph   May ... this is Eva Mason. Eva ... May Hassal.

May   How d'you do?

Eva   How d'you do?

Ralph   A young lady in a million or any number you care
to name. She can write copperplate as good as him and does
sums up to long division. And strong? She's a female Eugene
Sandow.

Eva   He does his best to embarrass me.

May   It's nice to meet you. I'm sorry you catch us at our
busy time with the world about to descend on us.

Ralph   Tom ... have you asked her?

Tom   Not in full. You see ... with me going off to
Caernarvon with the Pals ... the idea was that she'd like to
take over my early turn on the stall ... from tomorrow.

May   Oh.

Eva   She doesn't know!

Ralph   It's not just that Tom. (*To* **May**.) We thought he'd have told you. He said he had. We thought she could have his room. She's come from t'other side of Clayton-le-Moors on the strength of that.

Eva   I don't know where to put myself. I thought it was settled.

Tom   I'm sorry.

May   You'll waste your life being sorry.

Eva   This isn't fair to you Miss Hassal ...

May   Nor to you. (*To* **Tom**.) Dolly daydream. Couldn't you speak?

Ralph   She's worked on farms on the poultry and the milking. She's used to getting up early.

May   Has she? Well she doesn't want to be standing out here with her cases. Take Miss Mason's things and put them in the scullery, Tom.

Ralph   There you are!

May   And be quick. She can have your room tonight at any rate. There's no reason it should go empty.

Tom takes *the bags and goes off to the house.* **May** *sets up her scales and cash box.*

Ralph   What did I say? Straight as a die May Hassal.

May   And this is the man who calls me a Tartar.

Ralph   Now! Only once.

May   I am a bit of a Tartar, you'll find. You have to be round here. You have to breathe fire.

Eva   It shouldn't be thrust on you like this. I'm very sorry for it.

May   No ... I'd be glad of your help. Watch how it goes and try a turn tomorrow. Then you can see.

Eva   I've always wanted to get work down here. I tried for the mills but there's so many laid off.

May   Don't I know. I see it in my takings.

Ralph   Where's the work they should be getting making khaki for Kitchener's New Army? Hambledon, Helene, Broad Oak, Fountain, Paxton and Victoria ... all shut down for repairs. Repairs? It's nothing but a bloody lockout.

May   Don't pose as the worker's friend, Ralph. As a clerk you should be above such things. (*She knows how to tease him.*)

Ralph   Should I? I'm kissing that goodbye, thank God! I'll not push a pen any more.

Enter **Tom**.

Come on Tom. Let's get on parade.

Tom   I'll do my turn.

Ralph   Your last clog chorus.

Eva   Clog chorus?

Ralph   Yes ... you don't get that on the farm! You don't know what we're talking about do you?

He gives her a rub on the backside.

May   Take your hand from there please.

Ralph   And keep your mind on the fruit. I'll have a couple of pears.

Through this we hear the sound of street doors slamming, clogs clattering on stone cobbles and women calling out to each other.

Tom *weighs two pears for* **Ralph.**

Voices   Elsie! Get yourself down here! Wait on me Mary! If you're not down in one minute ... Mary don't go. You'll be late for Christmas!

May (*to* **Eva**)   Watch Tom on the weighing-out. Has to be done to a farthing and they always try to get the benefit if you're over.

Ralph *holds up the two pears suggestively.*

Ralph   Oh lovely! How perfect in form. How goodly to behold!

He gives one to **Eva**. **Annie Boggis** *comes on.*

Annie   Reggie! Come here!

May   Oh not this morning!

Annie   Come here at once!

Reggie *emerges with a half-grin of resignation.* **Sarah Harding** *clops in, her shawl around her.*

Sarah   Three small russets.

Annie   Where you been?

Sarah   That's all we needed ...

Annie   Where? Where? (*She takes a swipe at* **Reggie** *but he dodges.*) Stand still while I hit you!

Ralph   Play fair. Let him use his feet.

Annie   Shut up! You are going to stand still while I hit you. Will you stand still while I hit you? (*She takes a few more unsuccessful swipes.*)

Enter **Bertha Treecott**.

Bertha   Morning May. Can I have an orange? (*Seeing the fray.*) Oh lor!

Annie   He's defying me! Stand still! This is your mother telling you.

Tom   Russets, Sarah.

Annie   Will you stand still while I hit you!

Sarah   Putting us off our breakfasts!

Annie   Stays out with drunks. Yesterday he was tying doorknockers together. Pulled Mrs Hamilton's knocker right off.

Ralph   Did he be God? And her a devout Wesleyan!

Annie   Take your low morals to your own end. (*To* **Reggie**.) Come here! (*Spotting her chance she dives in and clouts* **Reggie** *repeatedly on the head*.) There! There! And that ... and that. And take that dirty grin off your face. Oh you bugger!

Reggie *makes a fast exit.*

Annie   Now he's made me swear! You witness he made me swear!

Ralph   Takes a lot to do that, Mrs Boggis.

Factory hooters go off near and far.

May   Thank heavens!

Bertha   Tom. My orange!

Eva   Did she have to hit that boy like that?

Ralph   Regular show that is. You'll see worse than that. Stand back for the rush. This is your clog chorus.

Sarah (*to* **Tom**)   And one for me.

Annie   Plums!

May   No plums.

A blackout as hooters and the roar of clogs reach a crescendo.

Lights up on the stall ten minutes later. **May** *and* **Eva** *alone clearing the baskets away back on to the hand cart.*

May   No. All I have against the Accrington Pals is that they've taken the best men.

Eva   They volunteered.

May   Why? Educated boys like Tom and Ralph. You don't need qualifications to be shot at! Let those out of work go. The work-shy. Those who won't do a hand's turn. God knows there's enough of them.

Eva   Ralph was that fed up with the office.

May   Is that why? Oh these men ... never happier than when they're arms round one another's necks, bawling good fellowship, in full retreat from what life's all about. Well Eva, what d'you think? (*She indicates the stall.*)

Eva   I should like to.

May   Should you? I've scarcely made ninepence this morning. It's hardly worth it ... but you have to be here. And the girls like to pick up a bit extra to eat when they're out of the house, for they get little enough at home. All the titbits go to their fathers and the brothers get what's left. So maimed or halt you have to turn out in rain, frost or pitch black. I used to think it was mad getting up to sell apples and oranges by moonlight.

Eva   At least you've people to talk to. Putting cows in the shippin or out weeding kale on your own you go queer in the head. You get sick of being with yourself. And now Ralph won't be coming up on his bike I'm desperate to get away.

May   You're ... not in any trouble?

Eva   Me? (*Realises.*) Oh no. We were always most careful ...

May *gives her a look.*

Eva   I mean to avoid that kind of thing.

She is not very convincing.

May   Dear me. I've made myself blush.

Eva   I'm just glad to be in town.

May   Well you can still see the fields from most of the streets, even if you can't see them from here. Accrington's a

site better than where Tom comes from. Oh the Hackfords!
They had such a dreadful outlook. And such habits. They
can be very vile in Salford. No, these are not like the slums
he knew. Not slums at all. Not this end of the street at any
rate.

Eva   I always wanted to be where there was a bit of life.

May   Oh there's life here. Only walk up there a few yards
and it's falling out of the doorways on you. There's nothing
much you can do here but you're in the midst of life. You'd
better know what you're coming into. It's no Garden of
Eden. People are not paupers exactly, though some of them
behave as if they are. Those with the newspaper up at the
front windows. You can't be so poor that you can't find a bit
of net somewhere. The smell from them nauseates and their
children forever runny-nosed with lice and ringworm and
God knows. Oh and at the backs down the entries where
Ralph lives … have you seen? There's a lake of water, if it is
water, as black as treacle and what's in it I don't know … such
dead things and live things. It wants a river of carbolic to
wash it all away. So that's what you're coming into and you
must decide. And it's only part-time as you know.

Eva   You make it sound very bad.

May   I wish it were better.

Eva   And I know I'm a poor substitute for Tom.

May   What makes you say that?

Eva   Only that you must be sorry to see him go. Ralph told
me how you went to the recruiting office and tried to get
him off.

May   Did he? Tom's chosen to go. (*Smiles.*) Go round the
back to first gate. Door's open. Put the kettle on. Wiggle
the raker a bit but not too much or it'll burn away. We'll be
comfortable for an hour. (*Indicates hand cart.*) Put that in the
yard where you can see it or it will grow legs and walk.

Eva *pulls the cart off.* **May** *laces up the covers of the stall. Presently she turns thinking about her attempt to get* **Tom** *released. We now go back in time to play that scene.*

As lights fade on the stall **CSM Rivers** *enters in his shirtsleeves, his collar turned down. He lathers his chin for shaving.*

Scene Two

May *moves slowly into the recruiting office.*

Rivers   Yes m'am?

May   I should like to see the officer.

Rivers   No officers present m'am. Will the warrant officer do?

May   If you please.

Rivers   That is myself m'am. Company Sergeant Major Rivers. Would you take a seat while I finish the remaining whiskers? Leaving them only stiffens their resistance.

May *is suddenly shy of him. She sits. Then she gradually gets impatient.*

May   It's about a young boy you've recruited today.

Rivers   Name?

May   I'd rather not give it at the moment.

Rivers   Would that be because he gave a false statement concerning his age?

May   No! He's very truthful. He's nineteen.

Rivers   Some would call him a man at that age, not a boy.

May   He's still an articled apprentice.

Rivers *wipes his face and puts on his tunic.*

Rivers   You are related to him.

May   Not ... yes. I'm his cousin. Second cousin. But his parents are dead.

Rivers   And you feel responsible for him. Well, that's a cold way of putting it. I'm sure that this young man is held very close in your affection.

May   He is an apprentice lithographic artist at Warrilows and he's thrown his future away!

Rivers   And you keep a greengrocery stall on the corner of Waterloo Street.

May   How did you know?

Rivers   There's not much I've missed in this town m'am since I came. I was very impressed with your air of competence in running it.

May   He helped me with it.

Rivers   And that helped him ... not earning much from his apprenticeship.

May   He's too easily swayed. He's let others talk him into this.

Rivers   These are upsetting times for us all. I can see you're surprised, me saying that when my job here is to imbue men with the spirit of duty and service. All the same I can sympathise. I was just on the point of retirement myself. Had in mind a little business ... not unlike your own.

May   I'm explaining his situation.

Rivers   He signed. Took the oath.

May   Egged on by others!

Rivers   Oh m'am. If you knew some of the men I've had to make soldiers of in the past. Dregs and peelings of humanity, some of them, though they stood up well enough in the end. But here ... they're paragons! Your mayor calls for seven hundred volunteers from Accrington, Blackburn, Burnley,

Chorley and hereabouts. They came in a matter of days ...
and all in such a spirit of cheerfulness and good humour.
The smallest town in these islands to raise its own battalion.
It makes me humble.

May   He was drunk. He can't take drink!

Rivers   No m'am. We wouldn't have allowed it. I see the
homes these men come from where they have loved ones
and are desperately needed. None were taken in drink.

May   I could pay the money back ... what he was given ...

Rivers   There's no machinery for that. None at all.

May   I could pay you! I've money I was saving towards a
shop.

Rivers   Then I advise you to put it to that use. There's
great satisfaction in keeping a shop. You have no one else
dependent on you but him?

May *shakes her head.*

Rivers   Then I will tell you what I'll do. I will make that
young man my special charge. Hand your responsibility over
to me and I shall not be found wanting. I shall be with him
in every present danger ... the darkest moments, you can
be assured. Everything I've learned that has preserved
me till now shall be at the disposal of one you feel so much
towards ...

May   I didn't say ...

Rivers   I shall be his very shadow.

May   But he's an artist. He's forgetful ... he's no soldier!

Rivers   That is my task.

May   He mustn't go!

Rivers   He must. And into my care.

May   I want to see the officers.

Rivers   By all means. They'll talk to you. They'll talk to you as though it was all a game … a sunlit meadow for bright-eyed lads to go running after honour and glory like happy footballers. But I don't talk like that to you because I believe that you and I have an understanding. I have more respect than to talk like that. Whatever I do is done with seriousness. I may say, with love. Leave him to me.

May *is spent and confused by his manner. Something about him makes her unsure of herself.*

May   But you don't know his name.

Rivers   I think I do. I think I do, madam.

May   Tom Hackford.

Rivers   Private Hackford. Yes m'am.

As **May** *goes … Blackout.*

Scene Three

The stall. Mid-morning. **Eva**, **Sarah** *and* **Bertha**.

Sarah   Where's that man? I get home specially to see him off and where is he?

Bertha   You just don't know them any more! They even walk different.

Sarah   Well they think they're it, don't they?

Bertha   My own father come round the corner and I didn't know him at first. They look so swaggery in them uniforms And Ralph!

Sarah   Him! I've never known a man with such a talent for turning up everywhere at once. And he's that full of farewells.

Eva   You mean kissing all the lips on offer.

Sarah   D'you mind?

Eva   No. Minding won't change him will it?

Sarah   But he's very good. He's said 'goodbye' twice to my mother and he can't stand the sight of her. Has Madam left you in charge then?

Eva   No. It's not settled yet. She's just getting some plums.

Bertha   I feel neither use nor ornament. They go off and do it all and I stay here and do nothing.

Sarah   You do a full shift on the looms while they'll be playing around in tents.

Bertha   They're going to fight the Germans.

Sarah   In Caernarvon? The only fighting they'll do is with those Welsh women. The advance party said some of them are that wild they can't speak two words of English. One sight of soldiers and they pour down from the hills in droves.

Bertha   Droves! Are they like that?

Sarah   I can't see my Bill putting up much resistance. Still, it'll be over before he gets his oats.

Bertha   Sarah!

Eva   D'you think so?

Sarah   I've heard that our royal family is having talks with the German royal family. They're related. Isn't as if we're fighting France where they've got no royalty at all! The main thing I've got against the Kaiser is that he didn't declare war three year ago. Because then I wouldn't have got a kid and got married.

Eva (*to* **Bertha**)   What would you do if you could?

Bertha   I'd be a nurse.

Sarah   What d'you know to be a nurse? It's all ladies going to be nurses. Ladies and horribles. Sick of seeing their photos in the paper. The horrible Miss Snitch seen here tending lightly wounded at Lady Snot's country seat.

Bertha   If I could, I would. Oh those awful, hateful Germans!

Ralph *enters and sweeps* **Eva** *up into an embrace.*

Ralph   It's Accrington Carnival and Fête. You can't get down the street.

Bertha   Did you hear Ralph?

Ralph   Poor old Arthur's in a state bidding adieu to his pigeons. Did I hear what, love?

Bertha   The Germans. There was a picture in the local from the *War Illustrated*. There were these British Tommies digging trenches in Belgium. Along comes a funeral procession from the village down the road ... all Belgium people dressed in black. All our men take off their caps and stand in respect. Suddenly off comes the lid of the coffin and there's two great Germans with a machine gun. Shot them all down!

Ralph   Don't worry Bertha. We shall send them home in coffins they can't get out of. Where's Tom? Tom! I asked him to do a quick sketch of you so I could take it with me.

Eva   Yes he did start it but I told him not to bother. He wanted to pack.

Ralph   What? (*Calls again.*) Tom! Out here with you!

Sarah (*uncertain*)   How d'you get two Germans and a machine gun in a coffin?

Drums start up in a neighbouring street.

Ralph   There's the Boys' Brigade. When we heard there wasn't going to be a band at the station to see us off, Harry Leatherbarrel says: 'The hell we'll have no band. Get the brigade out!'

Bugles play a march. The girls climb on the stall to get a view.

Sarah   Blow, boys … blow!

Bertha   Oooh! Frank's on the big drum!

Tom *has entered in full kit.*

Ralph   That sketch Thomas!

Tom *gets out a pad and pencil.*

Eva   Don't be so overbearing!

Tom   Sitting by the stall just as you were before.

The girls sing with the bugles:

Sarah/Bertha
I've joined the Boys' Brigade,
They call me marmalade.
I hit me bum instead of me drum
I've joined the Boys' Brigade.

Tom   Could you lay your left hand on the counter? More this way.

Ralph   My little pocket Venus! My rose of Clayton-le-Moors!

Sarah   Me next Tom.

Ralph   He's only time for one … as I have.

Sarah   Oh yes?

Enter **Reggie** *in Boys' Brigade regalia pursued by* **Annie. Arthur** *brings up the rear in full kit plus a pigeon in a basket.*

Annie   Run you daft thing. They'll be miles off! Slowcoach! Couldn't find his mouthpiece.

Ralph   Can you blow it Reggie?

Reggie *does a quick blast on the bugle.*

Reggie   You just press your lips, tight, like, and do a sort of farting sound.

Annie   Get off! (*She takes a swipe at him as he goes. To* **Arthur.**)
And you stand by and let him defy me! What are you going
to do to those Huns if you can't lift a finger to your own
child?

Arthur   Christ said …

Annie   Christ said suffer the children. *Suffer* them!

Ralph   You're in Tom's way. The artist is at work.

Annie (*delivering the word like an insult*)   Artist!

Sarah   Is it true that when you were at Accrington Art
School they let you draw girls undressed?

She is doing this to anger **Annie**. **May** *enters and stays to one side
watching.*

Tom   No. It isn't. They were draped.

Annie   'Draped' … well we all know what that means don't
we?

Bertha (*genuinely interested*)   No.

Ralph   It means covered up so you can still see everything.
Tom has the artist's eye. He can look at any woman … any
woman … and see her in the softly shaded form that nature
first bestowed.

Annie   If you worked like a woman works you'd have
nothing left 'bestowed' at all.

Arthur (*peering at the sketch*)   You have a gift Tom. A divine
gift.

Eva *comes over to see. The others gather round.*

Eva   I've never been sketched ever. What's it like?

Bertha   Isn't it wonderful!

Tom   The hands aren't right. There's a knack of getting
hands …

Sarah   But the face!

Bertha (*to* **May**)   Say he's clever.

May   I never denied it.

Tom   I'll finish off the shading when we're at camp.

Eva   I don't know what to say.

Ralph   Put your lips to it.

Eva   What?

Ralph   Put your lips to it and I'll treasure it.

Bertha   Oh go on!

Eva   Will it smudge?

Tom   No.

Eva *gently kisses the sketch. The others respond.*

Bertha   Oh how romantic!

Sarah   My knees have turned to water.

We hear the Boys' Brigade wheeling round the streets audible again.

Ralph   They're coming back round.

Sarah   I must see Bill … Goodbye Ralph. Be good Tom. (*She kisses them.*) Arthur, I'll kiss your cheek. Goodbye!

She goes.

Arthur   God go with you Sarah.

Bertha   Are you taking that pigeon Mr Boggis?

Arthur   Oh, I couldn't leave this one.

Annie   The others have gone to his brother Bert. I'd have plucked and stuffed them and put them in pies else.

Arthur   England's Glory. I call her that because she's a match for any bird. Now before we go I should like us all to stand for a moment in prayer.

Annie   Not in the street.

Arthur   It's God's street.

Ralph   Go on. I've shut my eyes.

Arthur   Well God. Here we are in Your town, in Your kingdom, in the midst of Your creation, which, despite these shadows come upon us, despite the prison walls of life that surround us, looks lovely yet. You smile, I know. For we are men without craft or guile called to do Your work in far-off places. Bless the women who stay, Your handmaidens, for it is they who tend our homes and loved ones now. Keep us in their thoughts as they in ours and our feet to the paths of righteousness, amen.

All   Amen.

Each has reacted in his or her own way, **Tom** *most embarrassed, torn between his unbelief and his natural politeness.*

Ralph   You should preach at the Ebenezer.

Annie   And would have if he wasn't such a muggins as to be a Primitive.

Ralph   Let's get the train. Shut the stall.

May   No. Leave it.

Ralph   You're coming aren't you?

May   You go Eva. I'll see to things here.

Ralph   But you've got to come.

May   Got to?

Ralph   Can't you ever stop – One hour! Tom!

Tom   Not if she doesn't want to.

An uncomfortable moment.

Bertha   My father'll wonder where on earth I am.

Annie   Arthur!

Arthur   Goodbye May. His ways are mysterious. He makes a worker of you and a soldier of me. His will be done.

May   Come home safely Arthur.

Bertha (*to* **Tom** *and* **Ralph**)   I'll see you at the station.

Arthur *sets off in soldierly fashion,* **Annie** *following with* **Bertha**.

Annie   Don't march! I'm not marching!

Eva *has been signalling* **Ralph** *to make amends.*

Ralph (*to* **May**)   Sorry I spoke. If you don't want to ... it's your pleasings.

May   Nothing stops. Nothing! Not for the Pals. Not for the war. Not if every man in the town went to it. You can throw whatever you like away for seven shillings a week. Not here. They'll feed you and shelter you. Not here. That has to be got every minute of the day. No one gets it for you.

Ralph   You're still the Tartar of Waterloo Street. Good luck to you May.

Ralph *and* **Eva** *go.*

Tom   Shall I chuck it?

May   What?

Tom   Shall I not go?

May   And go to clink?

Tom   I could run my head against that wall!

May   This is the mood you've put me in. It's no use me standing on that platform waving a hanky and singing 'Auld Lang Syne' or 'God Save the King'. I don't feel especially proud of myself and I wish I could do otherwise.

Tom   Shall I be able to drop in ... on leave?

May   Providing Eva's with me and you're prepared to sleep on the sofa. But not if the house is empty. Not again.

Tom   I must thank you for taking me in and all that.

May *takes an envelope out of her pocket and thrusts it at him.*

May   Put this in your pocket.

Tom   What is it?

May   Put it away.

Tom   Not if it's money.

May   It's four pounds that's all.

Tom   Take it back.

May   I wanted to give you something.

Tom *stares at her. The bugle band gets louder as it passes the end of the street.* **Tom** *suddenly tries to embrace her but* **May** *isn't able to respond. She pushes him away.* **Tom** *can't give in and struggles with her but* **May** *is frantic and strong. As the bugles blare they keep up this silent wrestling with one another. Finally* **Tom** *breaks away.*

Tom   Yes, you'll give me money! You'll give me money all right!

He goes to the stall, takes an apple, bites it. Then he takes the envelope she gave him and slams it down on the stall. Then goes.

May *is left trembling with fear at what they have done.Blackout.*

Scene Four

May's *kitchen, three months later.*

Eva *and* **Sarah** *enter having just got home from the mill.* **Eva** *lights a lamp.*

Sarah   I'm dying for a bit of warmth!

Eva   It cuts you right in two.

Sarah   Quick then before May comes back and finds me in her kitchen.

Eva *gets a copy of the* Accrington Observer.

Sarah   Lord how I've hated this winter. I's'll have to hem up this skirt again. I'm sick of slush and frozen feet. And me empty bed all these months. Just me and a bloody hot brick ... I'll go potty. I'll have to do something. I'd join some fat Sultan's harem to get warmed up again, I would. Silk sheets, boxes of dates and an emerald in your navel! Have you found it?

Eva   There's a bit about the Pals at camp.

Sarah   There always is. Read me the funny poem.

Eva   You might not think it funny ...

Sarah   Read it.

Eva (*reads*)
   Oh where are those Russians,
   Those hairy-faced Russians,
   Who sailed from Archangel and landed in Leith?
   Who came over in millions,
   Some say, sir, in trillions,
   With big furry caps and armed to the teeth.
   Pray where have you put them,
   Or shipped them or shut them
   In England, France, Belgium, or in Timbuctoo?
   For 'tis tantalising
   Thus daily surmising,
   Come dear Mr Censor pray tell us now do!

Sarah   Oh that's good! Who's it by?

Eva   T. Clayton.

Sarah   He's clever. And you know I've met plenty who believed it. There was a train driver who swore he'd seen them. A thousand Cossacks on Manchester Central Station ... and with snow on their boots. As though they'd send them over here.

Eva   But if you're never told anything. Mary Cotteril's brother was stopped putting word in his letters home about the rats and lice in the trenches. The officer said he had to put uplifting things about how cheerful they all are.

Sarah   Well I'd better relieve me mother of the kids though I'm certain I'm too tired to face them.

Eva   Stay a bit. Kettle's on.

Sarah   It's May's evening for seeing her paying customers isn't it?

Eva   Who?

Sarah   Don't pretend. The posh lot up Peel Park way. We know. If anything's in short supply ... sugar or caulies ... she buys off them she knows at the market and sneaks it off to her special ladies for a good profit.

Eva   She wants me to go up there.

Sarah   Don't. They should put that lot to work. With their Tipperary Clubs and their comforts for the troops. They've started a sewing and knitting circle for making sandbags and socks and the way they do them you can't tell one from t'other.

Eva *laughs, then shudders.*

Eva   Thank God the Pals are still in England.

Sarah   Miss him?

Eva *nods.*

Sarah   I saw a sailor, home on leave from the Warspite. He was walking with that wiggle ... you know how they do? I went ting-a-ling all the way to the bread shop.

Eva *suddenly hears something.*

Eva   May!

Sarah   Read something ... anything.

May *enters as* **Eva** *reads.*

Eva   'Pals Inspected By The Duke of Connaught. The 11th East Lancs, our own Accrington Pals made a splendidly disciplined sight ...' Oh May ... I was just going to make the tea.

May   I'll do that. Hello Sarah.

Sarah   I only slipped in on the way back from the mill to hear the bits of news.

May   You're very welcome.

Sarah *exchanges a look of surprise with* **Eva**.

May   Did you read her the poem, Eva?

Eva   Yes.

May   Oh isn't he good that man? And she's such a good reader. I saw crocuses in the park. That's a hopeful sign, isn't it?

Sarah   Well I was just saying how we needed an end to the cold ... and so on.

May   I had a word from Tom today.

Eva   Did you?

May   Well he doesn't write much.

Sarah   Oh they're shocking that way.

May   She gets reams from Ralph. No, Tom just says how he likes the Welsh people and how they all stood in a crowd outside Caernarvon Castle and sang hymns ... and he joined in. Tom singing hymns! He said he'd never heard such singing and, you know, he's got a very fine baritone voice. Oh Eva, if he were here you could do duets, for she sings beautifully. I shall have to practise the piano so I can play for you.

During this **May** *makes the tea.*

Sarah Wouldn't that be nice?

May   Will you have a cup?

Sarah (*surprised*)   Oh! Well ... no, thank you very much. My mother ... and I've such work to do. Endless mending. There's nothing left in the seat of Albert's trousers but mending. You end up mending the mending and darning the darns. So ... I'd better be off.

May   But do drop in any time, won't you?

As she goes **Sarah** *gives* **Eva** *a puzzled look.*

Sarah   I will. Ta-ta!

She goes. **May** *resumes her more accustomed style.*

May   It'll be a relief to her not to have to poke her nose in from outside the window. She can come and do it indoors.

Eva   Now you've spoiled it!

May   I have, haven't I? Keep trying to reform me. You never know.

Eva   Will you have a bun? I got some.

May   You see! Rolling in it now. How was work?

Eva   Awful. Foreman teases me.

May   Jack Proudlove?

Eva   Calls me the milkmaid.

May   Tease him about dyeing his hair.

Eva   He dyes his hair?

May   Didn't you know? Uses soot and butter.

Eva   Is he that vain?

May   Oh no. It's not vanity. It's so the bosses won't notice his age. Quite a few of the older ones do it. It's a hard life.

Eva   It is.

May   While I was out I looked at a shop or two ... the ones I've fancied taking on, you know. And suddenly it all seems more possible. I never believed the war would make a difference like this. There's money around. The mills are back ... engineering, munitions. And there's shops that fell empty in the hard times you could have for really low rents.

Eva   But you don't want it to go on?

May   Not to take Tom and Ralph, no. Just long enough so's I can afford the stock. We'll be singing round the piano yet. Round here they think I'm queer in the head having a piano. But I could never let it go. It was my father's. When I was small we were quite up in the world. Lower-middle class. My father used to say upper-working but mother said lower-middle. We lived in one of those villas in Hendal Street ... before it went downhill. But then Father got this notion of speculating in second-hand pianos and that was his undoing. Lost money on them. Lost his job at Paxton's through slipping out to do deals. Did all kinds of jobs after that. Oh he was a character! He once worked for a photographer's shop. Now lots of people who had photos taken never paid up. So, one week while Father was in charge of the shop he put all these people's photos in the window with the backs turned to the street so you couldn't see the faces and a notice saying if they didn't pay up by Saturday the photos would be turned round. Sparks flew then! He got the sack. But then my mother, who was a very simple soul, and danced attendance on him, morning, noon and night ... well when she died it seemed she'd secretly managed to scrimp and save a bit of money and it looked like Father and me might get a shop ... a piano shop. But he frittered most of it away. Then he rented the stall like I told you. Took me from the mill to help run it. He just wouldn't do that kind of work. Went into a depression. I ended up keeping him till he died. You won't pass any of this on will you?

Eva   Of course not.

May   I trust you, you know. He used to love Shakespeare.
Took Tom and me once or twice when the players came.
But he'd get drunk and whenever the actors got their lines
wrong he'd stand up and correct them.

Eva   They wouldn't like that!

May   They didn't! He'd be thrown out and we'd hide under
the seats pretending we weren't with him, hoping to see the
rest. Oh ... Ophelia ... Ophelia. And Tom's a dreamer just
like Father was. That's what worries me.

Eva   D'you think Ralph might forget me? We've scarcely
been going together three months.

May   If he forgets you then you forget him!

Eva   Can't.

She holds up her hands spaced apart.

D'you see that? That's the distance from his right shoulder
to his left. Am I silly?

May   Yes. If you want an honest answer.

Eva   Look ...

She makes shapes with her hands.

There's his arms. There's his chest.

May   I don't want to talk about them all the time. I have my
cash book to do.

Eva   I've made up my mind to be truthful. I could have
given the wrong impression. I have slept with him.

May   You don't mean it?

Eva   I wouldn't want others to tell you. So if you want me to
go.

May   You've given yourself?

Eva *can't hide a smile.*

May   Have I said something funny?

Eva   No. I just hadn't thought of it as 'giving'. If you'd seen him as I have.

May   Well, as you say he's got arms and a chest. They all have, haven't they? But I'm a bit shocked that you should think I'd want you to go whatever you've done. I'm not very experienced in that way. What I know about men you could put into a thimble. Still, I hope I'm not a prude. Yet there are facts. At Paxton's … they don't pay you what they'd pay a man, do they?

Eva   No they don't!

May   And never will. You'll always have the rags and tags. So, unless you've some form of independence you have to be dependent on some man or other. And if you lose … that … they won't look at you. But don't listen to me. There was only the once with them … and that I don't brag about.

She notes **Eva**'s *look*.

Oh not Tom! Before I knew him. You didn't think that? Tom! I could never spoil his life!

Eva   How d'you mean 'spoil'?

May   I'm ten years older! And how could I live with such a soft thing? When he first came and was at Accrington Station, just off the train, a Salvation Army man came up to him and said: 'Have you found the Lord?' And Tom says: 'No, I've only just arrived.'

Eva   What a shame!

May   Well, let's leave the subject. Tell me, while I think about it d'you know what Esperanto is?

Eva   Esperanto?

May   Is it that language?

Eva   I think so …

May I must find out. Mrs Dickenson, Alderman Dickenson's wife, had a chat while I was on my rounds. Amongst other things she mentioned that she was secretary of the local Esperanto Society. I didn't know what to say. I did feel a fool. Whatever it was it took her to Paris just before the war. I told her about you.

Eva Me?

May Your singing. They run concerts for raising funds. For the troops.

Eva Oh you never said I'd sing?

May I didn't push it. But you could get asked. It's the way to get on. When I think how my father and me came to this door with our furniture and I saw how mean and small it was with its broken quarries and dark little stairs and I said never, never, never will I stay. (*Pause.*) You get yourself ready for bed. I'll do my cash.

Eva I'm relieved I told you about Ralph.

May Are you?

Eva I don't like secrets.

She hovers. **May** *gets her cash book and settles down at the table.*

D'you think they are moving them from Caernarvon to Staffordshire?

May It's what it says in the paper.

Eva But supposing that they're just covering up that they're moving them to France.

May They wouldn't do that. If they were moving them to France they'd say nothing. They wouldn't make up a story. Don't start decrying authority like Sarah does. That's silly. You can bake your cake. He'll be here on leave.

Eva And Tom.

May No. He'll go to Salford.

*Eva goes. **May** remains finishing her books. She lowers the lamp.*

*By the tarpaulin on the fruit stall **Tom** is revealed in greatcoat and full equipment. He is on guard duty at the training camp. Silence as he stares ahead and **May** makes entries in her book. Then she closes the book, stands and, taking her lamp, goes.*

Scene Five

CSM Rivers *moves to **Tom**'s side. He speaks very softly.*

Rivers   Guard ...

Tom   Sir!

Rivers   Keep it quiet. Guard ... attention! Stand at ease. Easy. Are you, guard, fully instructed in the procedure of challenge and recognition?

Tom   Yes sir.

Rivers   Make your report.

Tom   Nothing sir. Just two men on bikes, sir, ten minutes ago.

Rivers   What kind of men?

Tom   From the village sir ...

Rivers   What kind of men?

Tom   Farm workers, sir. From the Green Dragon, sir.

Rivers   Without looking at your rifle tell me ... is the safety catch applied?

Tom   Yes ... sir.

Rivers   Now look.

Tom *looks at his rifle and realises the catch is 'on'.*

Rivers   Apply it. That's a chargeable offence, Private Hackford.

Tom   Yes sir. (*He applies the catch.*)

Rivers   We don't want you shooting yourself in the head. Shoot the enemy not yourself. You're on our side. It must always be second nature to know the state of preparedness of your rifle. Make it an instinct. We don't usually have the luxury of thought when the time comes. You've good visibility . . . clear moon.

Tom   Yes sir.

Rivers   Clear, but small. Remote. I've seen moons over the Sudanese desert you could reach out and touch. Have you heard from Miss Hassal?

Tom   Just a few lines sir.

Rivers   I trust she's in health?

Tom   Oh yes sir.

Rivers   Now guard. What can you hear?

Tom   Nothing sir . . .

Rivers   You can hear men sleeping. Seven hundred men kipping like babies . . . deep in the land of nod . . . all tucked up in their pits . . . and each and every one of those men is depending on your eyes and ears. That's what soldiering's about . . . comradeship. So that some night when you've got your head down you know that there's a man out there who'll look out for you, no matter what. That's where we're different from civvy street. No one can divide us from each other. What dismays an enemy is the knowledge that every man he faces on the other side is loyal and attentive to his fellow at all times . . . not because he's ordered to be so . . . but out of the love he bears his brother in arms. Guard! Guard attention! Guard . . . stand at ease! Guard carry on.

As **Rivers** *goes and* **Tom** *stands guard a light begins to grow around the table in* **May**'s *kitchen. Gradually* **Tom** *becomes aware of it.*

Scene Six

Tom *moves slowly towards the table. He looses off his equipment and places it on a chair with his rifle. He hangs up his greatcoat and, removing his tunic, places it over the back of a chair. All the time he is listening as a man does in a sleeping house. He sits at the table. From above we hear* **Eva** *and* **Ralph** *... muffled laughter followed by* **Eva** *shushing* **Ralph** *... then* **Ralph** *murmuring: My love. Oh my love!* **May** *enters with a lamp. She is in her nightdress with a coat over it.*

May   Can't you sleep?

Tom   I just thought I'd sit in the kitchen ...

She looks up at the ceiling, nervously, then sits at the table. Another burst of laughter from upstairs.

May   Whatever shall I do? I shouldn't have let them, should I? I said to him: Ralph it's eleven o'clock. He says: Right, I'm going and then trots off up the stairs! Oooh, he's got some face! I haven't shut my eyes. But it's funny too.

Tom   What makes you laugh?

May   That leg of the bed you mended. It's never been right. I kept thinking: It'll come off! It'll have them over! (*Pause.*) All these months she's been like a sister to me. I can refuse her nothing ... nothing at all. Yet it is wrong of them. I always thought there was more to her than there seemed to be when she first came. She's so 'open' ... no, I don't mean 'open' ... so 'level'. She'll sit where you are of an evening and I'll find myself doing all the talking. And she'll smile and she'll listen and she'll comment ... sensibly ... and all the time she's being exactly herself ... never putting on, or saying things for effect. (*Listens.*) Here ... are they asleep?

Tom   Aye. I think so. In the arms of Morpheus.

May   Morpheus? Is that what it is? Well, I hope they are for old Mrs Big Ears next door can put a cup to the wall and catch everything.

She gets up, uncertainly, then goes into the scullery and returns with some flowers and wire.

Shouldn't you try and get some sleep?

Tom   In a bit. What are those?

May   Nosegays. I've had an order for a wedding. Buttonholes and corsage. It's years since I did any.

Tom   Whose wedding?

May   Oh, not round here. Mrs Dickenson's niece is marrying an officer from the King's Own Liverpools.

Tom   I must pay you something, May.

May   What for?

Tom   Staying here.

May   Don't insult me. Your money should go to Salford to your aunt ... who must wonder why you spend your leave here and not there.

Tom   She gets my allowance. Hardly spend a bean at camp. You don't need to. That's the great thing about the army. You don't need money. Everything's found. It's an exchange. It's really opened my eyes. I mean it proves it ...

May   Proves what?

Tom   That money's not needed. It's not necessary. Not really. People think it is because they're too boneheaded to see ... that it isn't. It gets in the way!

May   Don't raise your voice!

Tom   It's a free exchange of skills ... of produce of hand or brain. That's what's needed. Not money. (*Indicates flowers.*) The skill you put into that ... to exchange it freely for that which you need in return.

May   And what do I need?

Tom *is stopped by this.*

May   Dreamer.

He reaches for a nosegay. **May** *is on edge and starts as he comes close.*

Tom   I should have picked you some in Staffordshire.

May   I always think of it as Black Country.

Tom   No ... not Penkridge. It's a picture. There's a lake. I've tried to do it water colour, but there's a real knack in getting reflections. I should get oils.

May   How much do oils cost?

Tom *suddenly takes her hand awkwardly.*

May   No ... no ...

Tom   They're up there.

May   I know they're up there. Girls used to be taught to show restraint. To be 'spiritual'. Now they say 'What use is it thinking like that any more?'

Tom   Then what use is it?

May   I must go upstairs and you should try to get some sleep in the parlour.

She goes to the bedroom door. She pauses.

Tom ... would you do a sketch of me?

Tom   Now?

May   No, not now. While you're here. You've sketched Eva ... but you've never done a likeness of me, have you?

Tom (*bitterly*)   How d'you want it?

May   What d'you mean?

Tom   'Spiritual'?

May   I said it was how we were taught.

Tom   As the Lady of the Lake ... or the Angel of Mons?

May   Oh Tom! Do you think me so silly?

May *comes to him. He clings to her.*

Tom   I can't draw spirit ... I can only draw your face ... and your body ...

May   If I'd only known you now! If I'd only known you as you are now. Why did you have to come here as a boy?

She takes his arms from her and goes off.

Tom *remains as lights fade.*

Scene Seven

Arthur *is revealed to one side of the stage. He is in uniform. His pigeon basket containing England's Glory is at his side. He speaks a letter he has written home.*

Arthur   'To Jack Burndred, 14 Waterloo Street, Accrington, Lancs. Dear brother in Christ, as you will have read in the local the Pals have moved on from Penkridge to the cathedral city of Ripon. I regret the change. It is a move from God's cathedral of green fields and trees to the cathedral of the bishops. However, Ripon is a splendid garden city and lit by the new wonder of electric street lighting. Surely when we make progress like this shall we not ask: where is the progress we should be making towards the new Jerusalem?

The Pals were inspected by Lieutenant Colonel Sir Archibald J. Murray, KCB, DSO, who said it was the finest Kitchener battalion he had ever seen ... and he has inspected not thousands ... but tens of thousands.

Thank you for asking after England's Glory who is in fine fettle and makes our feathered friends in the battalion signals loft look a moth-eaten set by comparison. Thank you also for the news from the works. I was indignant to hear how the masters were still behaving, but God sees them, how they have sinned in the unacceptable manipulation of piece work rates in the finishing shop. There is not a quarter of a farthing wrongfully withheld from working men that He does not see.

You ask how I can bring myself to take up arms. I say how can I not when my fellows do? We have failed to build Jerusalem and this is God's answer. It is His second flood, though now by steel instead of water. Who has been perfect in God? Not me, for one. Sometimes I think the Vale of Sorrow I have known in the circumstances of my life tempted me away. Please ask Ethel to visit Annie and do what she can for the little ones and poor Reggie.

Well, God has called me to the lists and if I fall let my death help to cleanse the world of its weakness. I will close with the words of his purest handmaiden, Joanna Southcott:

"And now if foes increase, I'll tell you here,
That every sorrow they shall fast increase,
The wars their tumults they shall never cease
Until the hearts of men will turn to me."

Yours in the sight of the Lord, Arthur Boggis.'

Lights fade on **Arthur** *and fade up on the fruit stall for:*

Scene Eight

Winter 1915. **Eva** *is at the stall.* **Sarah** *brings on* **Bertha** *who is wearing a tram conductress's uniform.*

Sarah   Have you seen this Eva? Have you seen what she's gone and done? (*To* **Bertha**.) Stand up straight. You're not standing up straight.

Eva   It does look nice on you Bertha.

Sarah   Nice? Look at her.

Bertha   She's aggravating me.

Sarah   Don't tell me you haven't noticed!

Eva   What?

Sarah   She's shortened the skirt!

Bertha   Not much ...

Sarah   Twelve inches off the ground! I thought I was going it with ten! You racy little thing ... and stop bending at the knees. If you're going to be fast, be fast. Flash your boots for us. Come on!

Bertha *does a quick kick.*

Eva   Oh and you took in the jacket then?

Bertha   And got in trouble for it. But it was that baggy.

Sarah   I thought it was for selling tram tickets not driving the male population mad.

Bertha   Me? Even my father says I'm better followed than faced.

Sarah   What does he know? Two pounds of King Edwards. I'll pick 'em myself.

Eva   Is it getting any better?

Bertha   Not much. The men are such beasts about it.

Sarah   Who are?

Bertha   Inspectors and drivers. Drivers are worst. Mine's forever slamming the brakes on to have me fall over. Won't speak to me hardly ... and they won't have girls in the rest room except to get our tea. Then they dock our pay cos they say we have to have assistance with the poles, turning the trams round at the terminus.

Sarah   Oh they would have to cheat you. Would you credit the way they go on?

Bertha   They say we're taking jobs off them and that we'll want to be drivers next.

Sarah   And why shouldn't you? If there's one thing that narks the men about this war it's the way it shows them up for creating such mysteries round things. My God! Providing both your eyes point forwards and your arms aren't stuck on back to front, anyone can drive a tram! Especially with their skirt twelve inches off the ground.

Bertha   I don't want to drive a tram.

Sarah   You rabbit! Still neither would I. I'd be a female lumberjack if I could ... in the Forestry ... if I hadn't my own burdens.

Eva   I suppose they're afraid really.

Sarah   Who?

Eva   The men. Of being displaced. Now there's conscription coming, if women take their jobs they'll have to go.

Sarah   So they should!

Bertha   They can take some that I know!

Eva   Yes but they have to face getting killed. We don't.

Bertha   What a thing to say!

Sarah   What about the munitions girls ... the girls in Gretna that got blown to bits that they tried to hush up? And getting canary through working with TNT so you're coughing yellow cud the rest of your life?

Bertha   You make me feel I've done wrong.

Eva   I didn't mean to ...

Sarah   Come on Bertha. (*To* **Eva**.) You! You get yourself stuck here when there's so much you could do.

Eva   I'm not 'stuck'.

Sarah   I bet her nibs doesn't think so. She's got you.

Eva   It's not like that Sarah. I'm perfectly free. And I'd feel perfectly content in a way. At least we're all together. If I think back to home now all I remember is the dark. Whatever you say, Sarah, we've got what matters most.

Sarah   Well I never knew I was well off!

Enter **Annie Boggis**.

Annie   Have you seen Reggie? Blast him, I'll break his flaming neck!

Sarah   Oh can't you stop harrying him for a moment?

Annie   Harrying?

Sarah   Every minute of the day!

Annie   Harrying?

Sarah   Forget I spoke.

Annie   I want to know what you mean by 'harrying'.

Sarah   Never mind.

Annie   Bertha! What does she mean?

Bertha   Honestly Mrs Boggis, I don't know what it means either.

Annie   I know what *it* means you goof! I want to know what *she* means.

Sarah   For the Lord's sake.

Enter **May** *with the hand cart.*

Annie (*to* **Sarah**)   Miss Piss! Well, your games are over. (*To* **Eva**.) And yours Mary from the Dairy. I see what goes on, broad as daylight. Still that's over now. Your games are over.

May   What games Annie?

Annie   I don't have to tell you. It's over. All over. It's come at last. They're to be shipped. Three weeks and the Pals'll be shipped off to France. Yes ... I can see you didn't know.

Sarah   Who says?

Annie   Town Hall. Mrs Henshall got it from the bobby this afternoon. I left Reggie in the house and went up with her to see if it was right. Shipped to the bloody slaughter the lot of them.

May   It's true. They're going.

Sarah   There was nothing in the paper.

Annie   When is there ever? We got Mr Tenkerton out of the clerks office. They've got it in writing.

Eva   I shouldn't have said I was happy.

Bertha   I must go ... Mother'll be out of her mind!

Sarah   The kids! Come on Bertha!

Sarah *and* **Bertha** *go.*

Annie   Now you'll see some 'harrying'. Now you'll be learned what it means. Oh you'll be learned! (*Calls.*) Reggie!

May *inspects the cash box.*

May   You've not taken much.

Eva   Have they got leave?

May   Apparently. Some of them. Oh he'll come. But I wouldn't blame Tom if he didn't. I think you're wiser than I am. Least you're not going to look back and think Ralph volunteered because you were cold to him.

May *busies herself with packing up the stall.*

Blackout.

Scene Nine

May's *kitchen some weeks later.* **Ralph** *is washing himself with soap and flannel in a tin bath.* **Tom** *is repairing one of* **May**'s *boots. He has a cobbler's last held between his knees and is nailing a new leather sole on to the uppers, a biscuit tin of tools and bits of leather to hand.* **Ralph** *starts to make waves.*

Ralph   Swim for it! Swim for the shore! They see the rockets from the stricken ship. The wild North Easter blows it to the fang-shaped rocks. They're lost! Then Grace Darling leaps to the oars of her frail craft. Pull! Pull! By God it's parky in here. Brrrr!

Tom   This is past mending with nails. It should be stitched if I had the thread.

He trims the edge of the sole with a sharp knife. **Ralph** *winces.*

Ralph Here! Keep a good grip on that won't you? Bloody hell! Eva! Got any more hot?

Eva *pops her head in from the scullery.*

Eva   There's a jug of warm if you're ready for rinsing.

Ralph   Hot, I said.

Eva   You've had all there is that I'm letting you have. May'll go mad. Shall I come in?

Tom, *filling the leather sole, flinches uneasily*

Ralph   I'm in my skin.

Eva   I know! (*Entering.*) You don't mind do you Tom?

Tom   Er … no. Carry on. I'll finish.

Ralph   Nothing deflects the craftsman from his task.

Eva   You do look a cherub!

Ralph   I feel a brass monkey. I'm starved.

Eva   No more hot. I'll soap your back. Lean over.
Isn't he lovely? Don't you think Tom? Isn't he perfectly
proportioned?

Ralph   Shut up! You'll worry him.

Tom   His arms are too short.

Ralph   What?

Tom   For perfect proportion.

Ralph   Too short?

Tom   If you look at Leonardo da Vinci's drawings ... the tip
of the middle finger reaches further down the thigh bone.

Ralph   Bugger Leonardo!

Tom   *goes out to the scullery for his cobbler's wax.*

Eva   Let me feel that hollow in your back. Hmmm. That's
mine that is.

She kisses him.

Ralph   The miner's dream of home!

She tips the jug of water over him.

Here ... my arms aren't too short are they?

Eva   They can't be can they? They get everywhere.

The back gate slams. **Tom** *reappears.*

Tom   Hey-up. It's May.

Eva   Oh no!

Ralph   Towel!

Eva (*calling*)   May! Don't come in. Ralph's in the bath.

May *enters briskly with a shopping bag.*

May   Ralph's what? Oh my Lord!

Unable to retreat, she turns her back.

Ralph   I'm sorry May, our bath's got a leak in it.

Eva   And this one's got a parsnip.

May   Has he taken all the hot water?

Eva   I've rationed him.

Ralph   Isn't there a bigger flannel than this?

Tom   I'll hold the towel.

He holds it like a screen in front of **Ralph**.

May (*to* **Eva**)   You're splashed. What on earth have you been doing?

Ralph   Only what my mother'd do for me.

May   Dry yourself in the scullery.

Ralph *gets out into the towel.*

Ralph   But it's freezing in there.

May   Well rub hard.

Ralph *goes.*

Tom   I was here … all the time.

May   Were you? Yes I can see from the chaos. All these bits Tom.

Tom   Won't take a moment.

He clears up. **May** *inspects the boots.*

May   Doesn't he do them nicely? I mean they're just for working in but I'd have had to have thrown them away.

Tom   Should have been stitched. They need some wax round the edges. I'll borrow some off Jack Burndred.

May   I'll pay for it.

Tom   He'll lend it. He won't take money.

He looks uneasily at **May**. *But she smiles.*

May   Don't be long.

Tom *goes*.

May   Isn't it good of him, doing that for me? Now ... what d'you think I've got in the bag?

Eva   What?

May   You'll never guess in a million years. A rabbit! The rabbit man was down the market. I haven't seen him in months. It was a miracle he'd got any left.

Ralph *enters rubbing his hair.*

Eva   That's a beauty!

Ralph   He's a big bruiser. By God that's a tasty feller.

May   Who said you were having any? Would you skin it Eva? I don't fancy skinning it.

Ralph   I'll skin it ... if I can share it. 'Thou shalt not muzzle the ox that treadeth the corn.'

Eva   Use Tom's knife.

Ralph   I will render it naked as a newborn babe.

May   How horrible! Take it in there.

Ralph *takes the bag into the scullery.*

Eva   We used to stew ours ... with apple and anything really.

May   Yes. Or we could roast it. Isn't he kind?

Eva   Oh he'll love skinning it, he will ...

May   I meant Tom ... with the boots. Glad I got something special. D'you know what I'd do if I could?

Eva   What?

May *hesitates.*

May   I'd make a stuffing for it. Breadcrumbs and suet. Mince if I had some. Oh there was a to-do in the market ... left me a bit breathless, I think. Never even thought to get a bunch of parsley.

Eva   Was something happening?

May   Just such a crowd, all piling in, buying things. Seemed like everyone had got Pals on leave. Then suddenly the clouds come very low, right down to the rooftops ... and for three or four minutes there were these huge drops of rain walloping down and splashing ... didn't you hear them?

Eva   That's right! I was in the scullery. Big as saucers!

May   Yes! And so icy cold. We all run under the tarpaulins for shelter, shouting and laughing like a lot of kids. People got talking to one another. They'd got sons home or brothers or husbands. Or sweethearts. And I don't know whether it was the crush or the rain drumming on the sheets ... but I got quite dizzy. I thought: where am I in all this? Where do I stand ... to him?

Ralph (*off*)   Shall I put it in the big pan or what?

May   Get him the meat tin.

Eva *finds the meat tin and goes out briefly.*

Eva (*off*)   Put it in this.

Ralph (*off*)   D'you want the head? (*Makes a scary noise.*) Whaaaa!

Eva (*off*)   Get on with it!

Eva *returns holding a little pan.* **May** *has remained stock still.*

May   What's that?

Eva   The head.

May *glances at the contents of the pan and screws her face up.*

May   Put it over there! I shall have to resolve this, Eva, or I shall burst. My mind goes round and round. I find myself annoyed that I can't cope. I'm not used to it. What does he think of me?

Eva   He loves you.

May   No!

Eva   Yes!

May   He thinks I'm mean and a money grubber and we're always at loggerheads over one thing or another.

Eva   You're the apple of Tom's eye! Ralph says so.

May   Does he talk about me at camp?

Eva   He gets teased about you.

May   Yes ... about me being a Tartar ...

Eva   No. They think you'd be quite a catch.

May   Oh do they! I suppose they think I'm worth a fortune. Well ... how do I approach it? Come on. What do I say? Shall I wait till you and Ralph have gone up and then I could say: It's too cold in the parlour for you. You're to come in with me.

Eva   Well, he couldn't resist that, could he?

May   Isn't it stupid to be in such an agony about it. And Eva ... I'm such a novice ... at my age! Will that make it difficult d'you think?

Eva   I don't know do I?

May   You could try and remember! Oh, I'm so glad I've spoken! I will not be a prude, Eva. Cast care to the winds, that's what we must do now.

Ralph *enters with the meat tin and skinned rabbit.*

Ralph   There he is. What'd go nice is some carrots and dumplings.

May   Carrots and dumplings would be wonderful!

*She pats **Ralph**'s cheek.*

Eva   Let's splash out. I'll go down for some mince. They'll still be open …

May   Good idea. You stay. I'll go. I feel like a bit of a run!

*Enter **Tom** running with **Reggie** in his arms. **Reggie** is streaming blood from the nose.*

Tom   Hey-up! Out of the road. Give us a hand Ralph. Hold him over the bath!

Ralph *and* **Tom** *hold the boy so that he bleeds into the bath.*

Eva   Whatever happened?

Ralph   It's a nose bleed.

Tom   Get a cloth! May!

May *is stunned.*

Tom   I said get a cloth!

Eva   I will …

She goes out to the sculley.

Reggie   Haaa! I'm choking …

Tom   Turn his head!

Ralph   They say push a cold key down the back …

Tom   Cough it out! Cough!

Eva *has returned with a cloth.*

Eva (*to* **May**, *indicating cloth*)   Will it matter?

May *shakes her head.* **Eva** *wipes* **Reggie**'s *face.*

Tom   Let him cough a bit more.

Ralph   Aye. Mustn't swaller blood. God isn't it red?

May   Can we know what happened?

Tom   He was sitting in the entry next door having a sort of fit. Look at this on his head. What she do Reggie?

Reggie   Used the strap on me, Mr Hackford.

Ralph   It's the buckle end, that!

Eva   Oh it's deep. Ralph, get clean water.

Ralph *goes.*

Eva   Hold your head back. Look up. That's right. Eh! You don't wear much do you?

She hugs him to her, warming him.

Tom   We'll need the iodine.

May   I'd rather you didn't.

Ralph *returns with a bowl of water.*

Ralph   He's looking better already. Takes more than a clout on the nut don't it Reggie?

Reggie   Her tried ter hit me agen but I got out!

Ralph   You'll get your Military Medal. Evasion in the face of the enemy.

Eva   Now hold still.

She bathes the cut.

Tom   Should have iodine!

May   Let Eva clean it up. Go outwards from it all the way round.

Tom   I've got my field dressing. We'll use that.

May   I'd sooner we didn't use anything. If we start bandaging it she'll only think we did it to aggravate her.

May *stands her ground.* **Tom** *and* **Eva** *are rebellious.* **Ralph** *is embarrassed.* **Eva** *tears a little square of cloth and presses it to* **Reggie**'*s forehead.*

Ralph   That's it love. That'll do the trick.

Tom   He should stay here.

May   Whatever are you talking about?

Tom   He's lost blood. He should lie up.

May   He can do that at home.

Eva   Why not here?

May   It's interfering. He's her son. I'll tell you what we'll do. (*To* **Reggie**.) You've got to learn to keep out of trouble, haven't you? I think you go out of your way to get paddled. You've got to realise the war's taken your father away and your mother's that worried. She wants some support from you. Now that's not bleeding any more is it? Keep that little square on, go home and tell your mother I've asked you to start running a few errands for Eva and me on the stall. And for that I have given you an apple (*gives him one*) and a threepenny joey. Eat the apple later. Not now for you may have swallowed blood and that'll make you sick. But make sure you show your mother the threepence.

Reggie   What shall you want me to do?

May   Do? There's no end to do. Show it her. Tell her I'll be round tomorrow to ask if it's all right. You understand?

Reggie   Yes Miss Hassal!

He goes.

Ralph   Clever woman! Eh? Brains!

May   It's nothing clever. I just think it's more sensible than inviting trouble.

Tom *moves suddenly. He puts on his tunic followed by his greatcoat.*

May   Tom, he's only four doors away. He can walk on his own!

He dashes out and returns immediately with his kitbag, stuffing things in.

Eva   What are you doing?

Tom   They're stuck! Stuck! That's why everything's cock-eyed. Stuck in their own little worlds. They can't see further than what they know. Mentally stuck. It's got that they think they'll go under for stepping beyond their own backyard.

Ralph   Who's this Tom?

May   He means me. When he says 'they' he means me.

Tom   No I don't. I'm talking of the general, not the particular. That's the trouble. They can't generalise. They have to bring everything down to the particular. If you try and explain the theory of the free exchange of skills they think you're talking Chinese! It's the same in a trade. They take on an apprentice and then tell him nowt. Scared stiff of anyone stepping over the line. Scared of imparting knowledge. Well, now they're worried. This war has got them worried. They're cornered. It can't be carried on without the free exchange, d'you see? Skills have got to be taught. It's all out in the open. And the dunderheads and numbskulls that lord it over here, they'll be seen for what they are over there!

May   Yes I expect it'll be wonderful over there. Heaven on earth for you. Why do you come here to turn on me and turn on me and go on at me? If that's where you want to be, go there. Get out of my sight.

Tom *hovers uncertainly, then grabs his kit.*

Tom   Ralph can wax the boots. He knows how.

Tom *goes.*

Eva   May, don't let him!

May   He has to challenge me …

Eva   Stop him Ralph.

Ralph   I'm blowed if I know what it's all about!

Eva   Put your coat on May. I'll get it.

She brings **May***'s coat.*

May   If he hadn't challenged me …

Eva   He'll be standing in the street wondering what to do …

May *allows her to put the coat on her.*

May   It isn't as though it comes from him … half of it's out of books! Or from other people. He thinks more of other people than he does of me! I've been behaving like a ninny …

Eva   Go after him.

May   There's not an inch of common ground between us!

Eva   Bring him back. Please!

May *goes, hopelessly.*

Ralph   Well it's put me in a right fog. I'm in pea soup here.

Suddenly **Eva** *goes to him, kissing him on the mouth, the eyes, all over his face, crushing herself to him.*

Ralph   Eh little Venus. What's this for?

Eva *breaks away.*

Eva (*indicating the bath*)   Help me get this in the yard and tip it. I'm sure there's enough blood and water and mess round here.

As *they take out the bath, the lights fade.*

Scene Ten

A light on **May** *at the stall, now closed up. She stands uncertain what to do. Thinking* **Tom** *might still be close she whispers:*

May   Tom ... are you there?

She senses a movement to one side.

Tom!

CSM Rivers *enters, muffled up in his greatcoat.*

May   Who is it?

Rivers   Rivers, Miss Hassal. CSM Rivers.

May   You should say who you are in the dark!

Rivers   I'm sorry. No intention to startle you. I was just taking a turn round the streets, saying goodbye to my family ... or 'adopted' family, I should say, since I've none of my own. That's my fancy, you see. Having taken so many of your menfolk under my wing, I like to think of their kin as mine. Well, he should make the Manchester train easy enough ...

May   Who?

Rivers   Private Hackford. I saw him on his way just now.

May *is caught unprepared for this.*

Rivers   Shine on Accrington! They can talk of duty and service at GHQ. They should come and see this. There's people here don't talk of it ... they *know*. They've faced the worst that could come with no defence, no cushioning, nothing but wearing out the way to work and back on long hours and short commons. People who've faced death already for their nearest and dearest ... and felt it coming round the corner and stood up to it one road or the other. But that's the valour of life and there's no medals for it. I don't know what those Prussians and Saxons and Woortenburgers think they've got behind them to stand against this!

May   He wanted the Pals and he's got the Pals.

She goes. **Rivers** *remains. As the light fades we hear, distantly, a low rumble of guns and machine-gun fire.*

Act Two

Scene One

The sound of machine guns, distant.

Ralph *and* **Eva** *are revealed.* **Ralph** *is in France. He is in full service marching order, exhausted from marching, leaning against the tarpaulin.* **Eva** *sits, quietly tacking the hem of a white muslin dress by lamplight in* **May**'s *kitchen.*

Ralph   Oh my dearest, my own little pocket Venus ... my rose of Clayton-le-Moors. This is no letter you'll ever get. My love. Sweet Eva. It's come. After God's long ages it's come and we're up to the line for the big push. But for the moment we're lost, as ever. Lost three times finding support trench. Now lost again. It's like a bake oven this summer night. I'm in a muck sweat. My sore throat's back. I've spewed my ring up twice. They say Jerry's beat but there's lads seen his observer balloons up all afternoon watching every move we made. I was ready enough once. Christmas when they sent us off to fuckin Egypt to fight Johnnie Turk. But he was whipped before we got there so I'd got myself ready for nowt. I was ready when they brought us back and into France. But it's been up and down, round and round, in and out, waiting and waiting till I don't know how I shall go at it. I've heard the flies buzzing out there. Every shell or bomb as falls short sends up clouds. Still, they're only old regulars lying out there, who, as May would say, are very low at the best of times. I've been a bastard to you Eva, if you only knew. Slept with whores. And one little mam'selle in Amiens who'd take no pay. I sat on her doorstep right after and cried for you. All I want to volunteer for now is a night raid on your bosom in a field of snowy white bedsheets. That's a fact.

The light on **Ralph** *fades. There is more light on* **Eva** *who begins to work on the dress with a sewing machine. The sound of the sewing* *machine rises above the fading away of the machine guns.* **May** *enters.*

May   Oh you've not!

Eva   It's not much

May   But I said I'd do it. For I know it goes against the grain. Still you're better with the machine than yours truly. It is not my forte. I shouldn't have worn this, it was too hot for me. (*Removes coat.*) And I think I've torn it under the arm. Am I getting fat?

Eva   You? Hardly.

May   There's a bit more than there was in the basement area. And Mrs Dickenson had such a lovely summer jacket in nigger-brown velvet with little tufts of squirrel here and here. I felt right outfaced as usual. How's the tea?

Eva   A bit old.

May   It'll do. They're all looking forward to hearing you.

Eva   Are they? Ooo ... er!

May   You'll be the prize attraction. And if this weather holds it will be so glorious. Her garden! Such immaculate lawns. It makes you wonder what you're living for. Such blooms!

Eva   Did you take Reggie in?

May   Now there I've got a confession. My courage failed me. I left him down the road in the park and carried the baskets myself. Isn't that dreadful? And I got a shock when I got back to him. There he was flat out on the grass. I thought he's had another do. But no ... he was right as rain. I said: 'What's the matter ... are you tired?' He says: 'No miss, I'm listening for the guns!'

Eva   Oh they all think that. Some put their ears to the railway lines.

May   The guns in France? He says there's been freak hearings in Yorkshire ... I says I'm not surprised. Are you finished?

Eva   Just a bit round the sleeve.

May   And I'll do the sash.

She gets needle and thread and a red, white and blue sash to sew.

The sunset was an absolute picture. I was standing gawping at it at the end of the street when up comes Sarah. She said you and she and Bertha were going to the Red Lion.

Eva   Oh yes. Yes we are.

May   No you're not.

Eva   What did you say?

May   You look as if you could murder me you do. I know you know what I think. And I know you think I don't know what goes these days. I said to Sarah: 'Get a jug and one for me and come round here.'

Eva   Here? You didn't!

May   Why not? Go to the pub and you're only on sufferance. You're either with the drabs or the fancy women. And Sarah's you can't go to for her mother being a misery all over ... and Bertha's brothers are pure purgatory. What are you staring at?

Eva   You and your hen party.

May   I'm not that inflexible you know. Anyway, I feel a bit like celebrating. Put the dress on. Let's see how it hangs.

Eva   Celebrating what?

May   Well ... the war ending.

Eva   Oh yes. One more push.

May   Put it on.

May *helps her as she removes her own dress and puts the other on.*
*Then **May** hugs her.*

Eva   Oh you are in a mood!

May   I shall have to tell you. I've found the shop. The shop
I've been looking for. Did you think I'd give up the idea?
I've found it and it's beautiful.

Eva   Where?

May   Somerset Road, if you know it. Across the park on
the other side. I haven't let on about it in case it was another
dead-end place. But it's perfection. High-class provision
store. Calls itself an emporium but it's not too big and
it's very reasonable. The man who ran it has gone to the
Manchesters and his wife can't cope.

Eva   Have you taken it?

May   Not yet. I've still to decide finally. The house has a
hot-water system. Back boiler! There's a proper bath and a
tiled range and a little bit of a real garden with a hedge.

Eva   It sounds marvellous. It is exactly what you wanted
isn't it? I'm so happy for you.

May   For me?

Eva   I can easily move in with the Henshalls next to
Bertha's.

May   Oh no! No. I want you to come in with me.

Eva   Well. It's a bit far.

May   From here? Of course it is.

Eva   I meant from work.

May   Haven't I made it clear? I want you to come in with
me. As a partner. Leave the mill. You don't need that any
more.

Eva   What d'you mean?

May   Share it. Live there. Divide the profits. Or pool all together. However you wish.

Eva   But I should need some money, shouldn't I?

May   I've thought of that. We pay the rent from the takings ... and for the stock and so forth, I'll lend you half and you can repay as we go, a little at a time.

Eva   I'm a dunce at money.

May   You are not a dunce at anything.

Eva   A bit of a wrench. I've made so many friends.

May   They can come and see us ... from time to time. Mrs Dickenson has given her word she'll patronise it. Some of her neighbours do already. We'll have a delivery boy with a bike.

Eva   Reggie'll like that.

May   Oh yes. Though give him a bike and it'd disappear in a puff of smoke. There's a copper beech tree just beyond the garden and I can see the sun shining on it and the rain falling on it and the snow ... such Christmases we could have ...

Eva   Aren't you good? Aren't you very, very good?

May   Oh I'm not out for goodness but an end to all these dark streets and rows and argie-bargies and niggling over tick and farthings off. There are more things in heaven and earth, Horatio ... Put on the sash madam and I'll get the things.

She goes off. Slowly **Eva** *puts on the red, white and blue sash.* **May** *returns with a cardboard Union Jack shield and a cardboard Britannia helmet and trident.*

May   Right. Hold your toasting fork! Other hand! Look dignified!

Eva   They'll be saying: Fancy her! Listen to that twang!

May   You have not got a twang. And you will sing like
Madam Patti.

Eva   More like Clara Butterknickers.

May   Please! This is the Tipperary Club ... raising funds for
our gallant boys. Oh there was a nasty moment apparently.
One of the ladies on the organising committee looked down
the programme and saw that you were singing 'Oh Peaceful
England' by Edward German. She says: 'Oh dear I don't
think we should print that word.' Mrs Dickenson says: 'What
word?' She says: 'German!' Well you know Mrs Dickenson.
She stood right up and said: 'That is an uncalled-for slight
on one of this country's most honoured musicians. Mr
German is as English as roast beef.'

Eva   So I'm still singing it?

May   Of course you are. Stupid woman saying that.

Eva   Haven't you forgotten Tom?

May   Tom?

Eva   Well ... you and me, sharing a shop. What about Tom?

May   What about Tom?

Eva   Say something about him ...

May   What should I say that isn't obvious? He's gone his
way. And I'm relieved he has. I'm enjoying life as I haven't
for years. And that's due to you. Not Tom. We can do as we
like. Get our meals as we like. I can get something for
you ... you can get something for me just as the mood
takes us. We're not forever treading on eggshells, being
touchy, afraid to speak are we?

Eva *takes off the things and gets out of the dress.*

Eva   I don't think you're being honest. I don't think that's
what you really feel at all. And I think you've forgotten that
when Ralph comes back if he still wants to I shall marry him.

May   Now what's this? I won't have you saying I'm not honest.

Eva   So is it that you want to get into this shop because you think the war's going to be over and the girls'll have nothing to spend any more?

May   I should not let myself be questioned by anyone else but you. But I'll admit there is something of that to it, yes.

Eva   And will you say that you want me there because if I'm there then Ralph may come there and if Ralph comes there then Tom may come too.

May   If you think that I don't want you for yourself and your company then I'm sorry. And if you think that I still want him dogging me and tugging at me and not letting me go ... leaving me alone to do what I so much wish to do ... then I'm hurt by that. You have hurt me!

Blackout. The sound of artillery barrage.

Scene Two

May *sits at the table, a little time later, doing her accounts. She will not be able to concentrate on them for her own thoughts crowding in.*

Meanwhile, the lights are brought up on **Tom** *in full kit standing by the tarpaulin. The sound of the guns has continued. The letter he speaks is one she will not get till later. She must never seem to react to it in any way. But, of course, his presence in her mind is very strong.*

Tom   'Dear May, just a few lines to thank you for the parcel. I hardly know what to say, it was so generous, all things considered. It bought you many good opinions of Ralph and Arthur and the rest, and not least of me. I hope you don't mind me sharing it as we do all parcels here. There was much praise for the kidney soup and strawberry jam, a most welcome change from our endless Maconochie and plum and apple. In return I hope to send you the

sketches I've done here of various Pals you will recognise.
What I have tried to capture in their faces is that free spirit
of comradeship you see out here but never see at home.
Despite the rough life it's the best feeling on earth the way
we're all for one and one for each. And that's lesson number
one for when this is over if we're not to go back to the old
narrow ways they force on us. I still have the snapshots of
you and will use my best endeavours to render your portrait
in crayon, though it can never live up to the good heart and
splendid appearance of the original. Yours in gratitude and
affection, Tom.'

The light on **Tom** *fades. He goes off.*

May *puts her accounts away. Suddenly the gunfire ceases.*

The lights go up in the kitchen area for:

Scene Three

Half an hour later. **Sarah** *and* **Bertha** *dance into the kitchen
singing at the tops of their voices.* **May** *has changed mood. She claps
her hands in time to the singing but her mood is somewhat forced.*
Eva *appears, pouring beer from a jug into a mug.*

Eva   Shall you have some more?

May   Of course I shall! Shall I have some more! Pour it out!

Bertha   Ooh! I do wish you'd stop feeling!

She has broken away from Sarah.

Sarah   You what?

Bertha   You know!

May   Sarah! What are you doing?

Sarah   Well I've got to cuddle something somehow.

Bertha   You are becoming awful.

May   I think you want a bucket of water over you.

Eva   Shall I fill one up?

Sarah   It wouldn't douse me. It's your fault Bertha. You look quite the little man in that uniform.

Bertha   I don't!

Eva   Someone doesn't think so ...

Pause. They look at **Bertha.**

Sarah   Who?

Bertha   It's nobody ...

Sarah   She's got a masher!

Bertha   I haven't!

May   You've found a young man?

Bertha   No!

Eva   He's an electrician.

Sarah   You've got an electrician? They earn a fortune! Where'd you find him?

Bertha   On the tram. He works on the trams. Comes out to us and does the wires ... you know. Well he rides on the platform sometimes. Doesn't really say anything.

Sarah   Too busy watching you go upstairs, you little goof.

May   Don't be so foul.

Eva   She's only jealous. He's proposed.

May   Really?

Sarah   Never!

Bertha   No he hasn't! At first I thought he was a bit gormless. Although you have to be clever to do his job, I know. But he'd just stand there grinning ... with his mouth half open, like this. I thought, Oh lor, I wish he'd go away.

Sarah   Get on to the proposal ...

Bertha   It wasn't. He just suddenly said in a very loud voice, 'Are you the marrying kind?' I said 'Are you speaking to me?' He said, 'Well I'm not speaking to her.' And that was so embarrassing because two seats away there was a nun. Well you know nuns when they've got their back to you, you never know what they're thinking.

Sarah   What did you say?

Bertha   Oh I said, 'I wouldn't marry you if you were the last person on earth.'

Sarah   Good. That'll keep him guessing.

May   He isn't one of these who wants to marry to avoid the conscription is he?

Eva   No, that's the thing. He can't pass the medical. He has asthma.

May   My goodness, I should think about it Bertha. Electricians with asthma don't grow on trees!

Bertha *sniffs and blows her nose.*

Eva   May ... you've upset her.

May   What have I said?

Eva   She doesn't want to think of it that way.

May   Oh? Are we so sensitive?

Eva   Yes we are! She's had an offer and she doesn't want it. Isn't that enough to upset anyone?

Bertha   Even if I liked him more I couldn't love him. I couldn't love a man who'd stayed at home ...

May   It's not his fault ...

Bertha   That makes it worse. If he was a dodger I could tell him straight. How could I face Father? Say he was wounded or gassed ... how could I?

Sarah   Come on! There's half this jug left. I'm not having it go flat. Drink it up. They'll soon be back. You've read what the guns have done. The Germans are blown to smithereens. Buried alive in their dugouts. There'll be none left to fight. The Pals'll be marching through the town and we'll be cheering ... and I shall have Bill back picking his nose and spitting in the fire and breaking wind fit to blow the ornaments off the whatnot.

May   Sarah! You're in my kitchen.

Sarah   Well it isn't holy ground ... is it Eva? Yes I fancied one of those tall bronzed Australians or Canadians but there you are. And what about Ralph. Eh Bertha ... eh? Back to Eva's loving arms. Oh Eva! Is he masterful? Is he passionate? Is he wild?

Eva   I sometimes think I'm the one that's wild. He can be very gentle.

Sarah   Not Bill. He's a steam-hammer. If he missed me he'd have the bedroom wall down! I used to get weary of being pulverised but I wouldn't mind now. Here's to loved ones!

Eva/Bertha   Loved ones!

May   Love!

Eva   Yes. Love.

May   You talk about love?

Eva   Yes!

May   It's all so sordid. So bestial!

Eva   Don't you say that!

May   I shall. I shall. I don't care what you think of me for it. I don't. Oh no ... not you, Eva. I don't mean you. I envy you. You just sail right through it. It doesn't seem to affect you.

Eva   What doesn't?

May This mean, dirty foul-mouthed place.

Sarah I see ...

May Where's love round here? Men round here ...
ignorant, stony-faced callous oafs, sitting in the best chair
waiting to be fed, like overgrown babies. Big fat cuckoos in
the nest. I'll tell you what love is to them.

Eva Some are different.

May Some? Yes, there's the silly and stupid side of it. You
so hope there's someone who'll rise above it that you're
ready to deceive yourself over fools ... thinking other
people are what they're not and never will be. There's just
everything to be done before you can even think of love. Oh
God I'm drunk. I'm drunk! Drunk! I shall put this aside,
Sarah, thank you very much ... and I shall go to bed. Good
night, good night, good night.

She goes.

Sarah You'll have to do something. You'll have to part.

Bertha I feel a bit sick.

Sarah (*to* **Bertha**) Come on. Fresh air. (*To* **Eva**.) You'd be
very well liked round here if it wasn't for that one. D'you
know? Move out. Don't tell her. Just move out.

Eva I can't. Not just yet anyway.

Sarah Oh not that bloody Tipperary concert. Don't show
up.

Eva I must. If I didn't ... I don't know what she'd do.

Blackout as they go.

Scene Four

Western Front, the Somme. The height of the artillery barrage.
Flashes in the darkness. Against the tarpaulin we see **Tom**, **Ralph**
and **Arthur** *crouched down in full kit, trying to stop the noise from*
their ears. The stage begins to lighten. Suddenly the barrage stops.
We hear the birds singing. **Tom** *and* **Ralph** *rise slowly.* **Arthur**
remains in some kind of trance. Now we hear occasional bursts of
fire from the German guns.

Ralph   Not in daylight! Not in bloody daylight! Why leave
it so late? We could have gone over in the dark. They'll see
us all now!

Voice (*off*)   Stand by!

Voice (*off*)   Close up Nine Platoon! Iggery, iggery!

Tom   Every man should have two jobs.

Ralph   Hitch my big pack up Tom ...

Tom (*hitching the pack as* **Ralph** *loosens straps*)   No one
should be stuck for ever in one boring job. We should all
share the tedious work and the interesting work.

Ralph   Fuck! I've broke this nail. Loose this strap will you?

Tom *does so.*

Ralph   If I'm in a shell hole I'm going to be out of this like
greased shit. The water in them holes can drown you.

Tom   It needs thinkers in charge, not thick heads. Rational
men. Men who have proper regard for the thoughts of
others. Readers. Men who've taken the trouble to read what
the thinkers have to say.

Ralph   I'm not going to drown. Shot or blown to bits but
not drowned. Loose your straps. I reckon if you're out of
your pack quick enough and get it under your feet you
might keep up. But tie your water bottle separate. Fuck all
use not drowning if you die of thirst! Oh these straps. I'll
never get out fast enough.

Tom   You could cut them.

Ralph   I've tried. Bayonet's too blunt!

Tom   Borrow this.

Ralph   That's your leather knife ... What will you do?

Tom   Oh aye ...

Ralph   What you made of Tom? You going over there to talk philosophy with them?

Tom   There's a lot of good German philosophers.

Ralph   Well there's fuck all of them over there! Wake up Arthur, get up.

Voice (*off*)   Move up Nine Platoon. Move!

Arthur (*to his pet pigeon England's Glory*)   Now sweet ... now my beauty ... the sun is shining and the air is clear ...

Ralph   Hold on to me Tom. Oh Mother, I've got the movies. Push me if you see me falling back ... don't let them see me go back. Christ I'm clasped so tight I'll bust!

CSM Rivers *dashes in to join them.*

Rivers   Heads down! Get your heads down! Seven thirty ack-emma ... mines detonating.

Voices   Stand by! Stand by! Take cover!

Rivers   Brace yourselves!

A vast deep roaring sound as the Hawthornden Ridge mine goes off. They cower and sway as the shock waves go through the trench.

Well the Pals! Next stop Serre for Beaumont Hamel, Bapaume and Berlin! (*Shouts off.*) Mr Williams, sir! Move your platoon up! (*Quietly to* **Tom**.) Think of her, shall we Hackford ... think of her? If you lose your officers don't make for the gaps in the wire ... Jerry's got his Spandaus trained on the gaps and he'll rip you to pieces ... cut your own; understood? Got your wire cutters?

Tom   Yes sir.

Rivers   Let glory shine from your arseholes today boys.
Rise on the whistle ... dress from the right ... rifles at the
port ... go steady and we'll be drinking schnapps and eating
sausages by sundown. Boggis ... let's have a prayer.

Arthur   Oh God ... do you smile still? Do you smile to see
your handiwork?

Whistles begin to blow around the theatre, merging into one another.

Rivers   Over we go ... stay in line ... right marker!

Voices   Come on the Pals. Up the Accringtons! Nine
Platoon! Ten Platoon! With me, with me, with me! Dress
from the right. Leave that man! Leave him!

They go over the top.

*Mingling with the machine guns stuttering we hear an awkward,
heavy piano introduction to Edward German's 'Oh Peaceful
England' being played.*

Eva *appears in her Britannia costume. She is singing at the fundraising concert. She looks tense and nervous ... almost angry. She
begins to sing.*

Eva
  Oh peaceful England, while I my watch am keeping,
  Thou like Minerva weary of war art sleeping.
  Sleep on a little while and in thy slumber smile.
  While thou art sleeping I my watch am keeping.
  Sword and buckler by thy side, rest on the shore of battle-
  tide,
  Which like the ever hungry sea, howls round this Isle.
  Sleep till I awaken thee, and in thy slumber smile.
  England, fair England, well hast thou earned thy slumber,
  Yet though my bosom no breastplate now encumber ...

*Suddenly she breaks off. She's lost the next line. The accompanist
falters.* **Eva** *begins to shake with fury at the situation she's put
herself in. She exclaims something and runs off.*

Scene Five

Sarah Harding's *backyard. She is pegging out washing. Offstage* **Annie** *calls for her son. She gives the customary low note on the first syllable, followed by a long drawn out falsetto scream on the second:*

Annie (*off*)   Re-hhh-gggeeee! Re-hhh-gggeeee!

She enters and repeats the cry. She is in her own backyard next door.

Sarah   Oh please Annie don't ... please don't ...

Annie   He's not hiding in your yard is he?

Sarah   No. He isn't.

Annie   I bet he is.

Sarah   I tell you he isn't.

Annie   He'd better show himself quick. I want him!

Sarah   Yes, I heard you say so. Well I haven't seen him.

Annie   Right. Re-hhh-gggeeee!

Sarah   Oh come on round and look if you're that suspicious.

Annie   I'll take your word for it ...

Sarah   Come round! Back gate's open ... come and look.

Annie *moves round to her. She looks in vain.*

Annie   Well where is he then?

Sarah   I don't know. Is he with Eva at the stall?

Annie   Eeeee-vvaahhhh!

Sarah   Give over! My head's like suet pudding.

Annie   And whose fault is that?

Sarah   That beer was off. I swear it was. It looked a bit cloudy from the start. He's no right serving it in that condition. I feel like my father when my mother used to say:

'Put your head under the tap, Bernard, your eyes are like piss-holes in the snow.'

Reggie *sneaks quietly onstage, sidling towards safety.*

Annie   There! There you are! Come round here. Come into Mrs Harding's.

Sarah   Annie, I've got to do this ...

Annie   It won't take a moment. Come on. I'll not keep telling you ...

Reggie *moves a little closer.*

Annie   Yes, I'm not surprised you keep your distance you devil! The bobby's been at the door. Bobby Machin's been round for you. They'll have you in the cells ... locked up in the dark with nowt to eat ... they will!

Sarah   What's he done then?

Annie   He was caught learning a gang of the little ones how to fish in the canal.

Sarah   Is that all? I'm astonished Bobby Machin said a word then. If he catches them he usually passes his helmet round for ha'pennies.

Annie   I'm trying to learn him to act right! Anyway it wasn't all ... was it you filthy animal? See ... he thought I wouldn't know the rest. Bobby Machin told me. He was getting those little children ... those little nine-year-olds oooh you beast ... getting them to repeat a rhyme after him. Look at him. He knows what I'm talking about.

Sarah   Surely it's not the end of the world ...

Annie   You can hear it. Because he's going to say it. He's going to stand there till he's said it out loud. You dirty-minded mongrel ... you're going to say it in front of Mrs Harding, now!

Sarah   I'm sure 1 don't want to listen ...

Annie And just the first bit ... d'you hear? Just the first bit. Say it. Say it.

Reggie (*mumbles*) I wish I was a little mouse ...

Annie Louder!

Reggie I wish I was a little mouse ...

Annie And the next bit ...

Reggie To run up mother's clothes ...

Annie That's it! No more!

Reggie And see the hairy tunnel ...

Annie Enough!

Reggie Where dadder's chuff-chuff goes!

She runs at him to take a swipe but **Reggie** *is off.*

Annie I said enough! (*To* **Sarah**.) I only meant you to hear the first bit. (*After* **Reggie**.) You wait! You wait!

Sarah It's a long time since I heard that one.

Annie You've heard it?

Sarah And so have you.

Annie I have never listened to that sort of thing in my life!

Sarah Haven't you? I used to wring it out of my brothers. All them songs they used to start off and not finish. I used to shut them in the bedroom till they told me.

Annie Oh what I have to contend with! And if Arthur was here all he'd say is: 'Follow Jesus.' What good's that to kids?

Sarah Well, if we all followed Jesus we wouldn't have any kids.

Annie What?

Sarah He didn't, did he? None that they mention in the Bible anyway.

Annie *is shocked but has to laugh.*

Sarah   That's better.

Annie   Only you could say that!

Sarah   I dare the thunderbolt I do.

Annie   If I'd known what was going to happen in my life. I know what people think about me. I'm weary. I'm weary of it all.

Bertha *runs on with a copy of the* Accrington Observer.

Bertha   It's here! It's over! We've won!

Sarah   Won what?

Bertha   The war! (*Calls off.*) Eva! May! We've won! I've got the paper. We're through the lines!

Sarah   Read it.

Bertha   'British offensive ...' No, I can't. I'll just shout to my mother and get May and Eva ...

She runs off shouting.

(*Off.*) May! Eva! Is my mother there?

Annie   What's it say?

Sarah   'British offensive begins. Official. Front line broken over sixteen miles.' Oh Jesus forgive me!

Enter **May** *and* **Eva.**

May   Is it over? Just tell me if it's over.

Sarah   The Germans are running ...

Eva   Read it!

Sarah   I'm trying ... 'Front line broken over sixteen miles. The push that could end the war has now been launched. British and Empire infantry are now in possession of German trenches, their exhausted occupants decimated by continuous shellfire over the past weeks. Those not killed are falling back in disorder as our victorious troops press home their advantage.'

Bertha *returns breathless.*

Bertha   Didn't I tell you …

May   Read it!

Annie   Does it mention the Pals?

Sarah   You read it Eva …

Annie   Are the Pals in it?

Eva   'Preceded by a bombardment of an hour and a half such as Armageddon had never seen' … Nothing about the Pals yet … (*Opens paper.*) Ah! 'Some of the battalions opened their advance by kicking a football ahead of them. They went over cheering as at a Cup Final' … no … no … 'Censorship will not allow the actual units to be named' … they won't say.

Bertha   We're through! We're through!

May   Is there more?

Eva   'Only a handful of the German machine-gunners were left to man their posts. Fire was wild and panic-stricken, though, inevitably, some of our brave soldiers fell here and there … refusing help and urging their comrades on.'

Annie   They don't say any more?

Eva   No. No details. Or names.

Bertha   I don't know where mother's got to. Oh what a relief … after all this time!

May (*to Eva*)   Let me have it please.

Annie   He'll not have had the sense to keep out of it. His back could have kept him out.

Sarah   Come on Annie … it's victory! 'God save our gracious King.'

Bertha   Hurrah!

Sarah   I'm glad I put the flags out ...

She holds a pair of drawers against her.

Up the Pals!

Annie   Yes. That's your flag, that is!

Sarah   Well ... there's a few battles been fought under it I admit! I've got a little drop of gin hidden in the scullery. I'll get it.

She hands the drawers to **Eva** *and goes.*

Peg 'em up for me love.

May   'More detailed information will become available in the next few days ...'

Bertha   I thank God. I thank Thee God ...

Eva   Could you hand me a peg?

Bertha   Oh yes.

Annie   I wouldn't touch her bloomers with a bargepole.

Bertha   What's the matter Eva?

Eva   Thinking.

Sarah *returns with the gin.*

Sarah   Shall I pass it round?

Annie   No thanks.

Eva *and* **Bertha** *share it.* **May** *shakes her head as she leafs through the paper.*

Sarah   The Pals ...

May   Oh there's a paragraph about the concert.

Eva   I don't want to hear it.

May   I'm going to read it.

Eva   No.

May   But it's wonderful! 'It was a great emotional climax to the evening when Eva Mason as Britannia rendered Edward German's "Oh Peaceful England" with such purity and nobility of tone … and it was surely fitting that the singer herself was so overcome that she was unable to complete the final lines of the song. This spontaneous demonstration of true feeling left no eye unassailed by tears!'

Sarah   I thought you said you'd forgot the bloody words!

Eva   I had!

May   Never mind. You triumphed.

Bertha   Isn't that funny?

Eva   So much for papers!

During this, at some point, **Annie** *has spotted something offstage that holds her attention.*

Annie   What's that over there …

Sarah   Are you mentioned May?

May   Yes, I'm listed amongst the helpers, next to Mrs Henry.

Sarah   Oooer!

Annie   That bird. Will you look at it Sarah?

Sarah   Where?

Annie   On our coal-house roof.

Sarah   I can't see anything …

Bertha   Oooh. My head's in such a whirl …

Annie   Shut up! It's coming back over the ridge. There with its wing hanging down …

Sarah   That pigeon?

Annie   It's come back.

May   What are you talking about?

Annie   D'you think I don't recognise it? It's come to the coop.

Sarah   You haven't got any pigeons ...

Annie   It's his! It's England's Glory.

Sarah   Don't be daft!

May   What is it?

Sarah   She thinks it's the bird Arthur took to France. It can't possibly be!

Annie   See. It's dragging one wing. Oh God! It's got blood on it!

Bertha   No. It couldn't have flown all this way ...

Eva   Oh surely you're mistaken ...

Annie   I'm not. It's finding its perch.

Sarah   It's one of George Deakin's. They're always round pecking for bits. Ugh! I can't stand feathers ... them thin little bodies all puffed out ... Shooo!

Annie   Don't! It'll go into coop.

They all watch fascinated, catching **Annie**'s *mood. Suddenly they start back.* **Sarah** *screams.*

Sarah   I'm not going to look ...

Bertha   It'll fall ...

Eva   It's half dead ...

May   What's it doing, edging down the roof like that?

Annie   It's England's Glory. I daren't put a foot in there. Will one of you get it?

Sarah   Oh Lord. No!

Annie   One of you go.

May   Whatever for?

Annie   See if there's anything with it. If there's a thing on its leg.

Eva   I'll go. I'm used to birds. Can I take your bucket, Sarah?

Sarah   What for?

Eva   To put it in.

Sarah   No! Oh all right.

Eva *goes off with the bucket.*

May   It's just some stray that a cat's worried and let go of ...

Annie   Tell her there's a sack in the coop. She can cover it over with ...

Bertha   Eva. Cover it with the sack out of the coop!

May   You mustn't give way to imaginings.

Annie   Don't tell me I'm imagining! I felt it would come many a time. I've laid awake thinking I'd see it in the morning.

Bertha (*calls*)   Be careful!

Sarah   Oh my stomach!

Bertha   She can hardly reach it ...

Sarah   Eva ... don't! Don't let her bring it in!

Sarah *retreats as* **Eva** *enters nursing the bucket with the sack over it.*

Eva   It's an awful mess ...

Sarah   Keep it under! Don't let it get out ...

Eva   It's dying ...

Annie   Never mind that. What's it brought?

Eva   Nothing ...

Annie   Its leg. On its leg!

Eva   Just a clip ... and a number.

Annie   Nothing else?

Eva   No. Nothing.

Annie   Get rid of it. Burn it. Put it on the fire!

Sarah   Take it away!

Eva   Poor thing. Heart's hardly beating. I'll drown it.

She goes. **Annie** *sways.*

May   Sarah ... get a chair for her.

Bertha   Mrs Boggis! There wasn't anything.

Annie   It's the end for me.

May   Talk sense.

Annie   It's the last I'll do.

Bertha   Shall I get smelling salts?

Annie   I can't see. Where are you? Are you there or not?

Sarah   Have a little drink of this ...

Annie   No! I'll not drink! I'll not eat ... I'll not do nowt.

Reggie *enters quietly, unobserved.*

Annie   The fool's dead. So he's dead. I never wanted him in the first place. I would never have had him if that soft halfwit thing hadn't been born and I had to have someone! I'd have never had his. But I'll do nothing for them now. His mother can care for them. Not me. They say I nearly died of scarlet fever when I was four. I wish I had!

She flings herself down, crawling. **Eva** *enters.*

Bertha   Oh don't Mrs Boggis, please.

Annie   I shall eat stones. I shall eat stones ... that's what I'll eat now ...

Eva   Let's get her home.

Reggie *comes forward.*

Reggie   I'll do that. Stop staring at her!

Annie (*clinging to him*)   Oh Reggie. You're the one who's mine.

Reggie   Stop making a show. Get up. Stop staring!

Annie   You won't go will you? You won't go. Where is this? Where is it? What's that wall? There's a brown gate. I don't know any brown gate ...

Reggie *helps her offstage, slowly.*

May   Well how silly to let yourself go like that. And say things like that. I always thought she had a bit of sense. As though that bird could have come from France. As though it meant anything if it did.

Bertha   That's what I think ...

Sarah   I hate birds ...

Eva   Let me borrow your little shovel Sarah. I'll go and bury it.

Scene Six

A day later. **May**'s *kitchen.* **Eva** *enters wearing a shawl and carrying a small bag and a bunch of flowers. She listens for* **May**. *Silence. She takes a chair and places it carefully and sits staring at a spot on the floor, still holding the flowers. She thinks of something and her eyes turn towards the kitchen. She lays the flowers on the table and goes off a moment.*

She returns, dragging the long tin bath. She places it just where it was when **Ralph** *bathed in it and kneels by it. She reaches out* *to the invisible form of* **Ralph** *in the bath and touches him, on the shoulders, down the arms, round the chest. Then, as she sits, staring, slowly fade lights to dim. After a while* **May** *enters.*

May   Oh! You frightened me. Eva? Eva …

She goes off and returns with the lamp.

Sitting in the dark?

Eva   It wasn't dark.

May   You really mustn't dwell on things that have no foundation. There's work to do. We have to plan. I've seen Mr Brownlow in the market. He's interested in the stall for his niece … though he won't agree a price yet. Are you going to use that bath or what?

Eva, *furious, drags the bath away to the scullery, offstage. Presently she returns.*

May   If you're going to lose your temper with me maybe we'd better not speak. You've changed.

Eva   Yes. I've lost Ralph.

May   Oh this is so foolish. I've looked in on Annie. She's had a temporary relapse. But in moments she has her wits about her and she's very sorry she's caused anyone to worry. I've brought you the paper.

Eva   I don't want to see it …

May   There is absolutely no report of the Pals being in the advance. The casualties so far are mostly lightly wounded and very few killed …

Eva   They're lying.

May   Why should they lie?

Eva   For their own ends … I don't know why. They take it on themselves to decide what we hear about and what we don't. Haven't we proved it over and over? Go out in the street and ask. They all believe the Pals were there. Why should you be the one that doesn't?

May   There's no law that says you must go along with the herd!

Eva *moves quickly towards her with her hand raised. She stops herself*

May   You'd do that to me? Then you can go as well.

Fade to blackout.

Scene Seven

There are lights on the stall. **Reggie** *pushes on the hand cart. He is tense and close to tears. He works quickly, undoing the tarpaulin, setting out the baskets.* **May** *appears with her scales and money bag.*

May   Now I told you not to come.

Reggie   Gran's round to put her to bed.

May   But it's you your mother needs. I thought she was improving today.

Reggie   Her started screaming again.

May   Oh dear, did she? She must get a good night's sleep.

Reggie   Her wanted rug out of kitchen burnt. We had to hide it.

May   Why?

Reggie   Her said it was all muddy and bloody.

May   Oh what next?

Reggie   Her thinks her saw Father standing on it. He come in through front door, her says. Stood on rug wi' a big hole here … in his neck, dropping blood.

May　It's only what she's saying. Take no notice. She'll get over it. He's not dead. We'll mix a few nice things up for her.

Enter **Bertha**.

Bertha　Oh May have you seen Sarah?

May　Not since this morning.

Bertha　I knocked at her door. She wasn't back.

May (*to* **Reggie**)　Take them. Make sure she has her sleeping draught. If you need me shout for me.

Reggie　Thank you, miss.

He goes.

Bertha　That's funny. She set out before me. She went to the station. I went to the Town Hall.

May　What for?

Bertha　To see what we could find out.

May　Turn that lamp down for me love, or I'll be had up for showing too much light.

Bertha　There was quite a few at Town Hall, but they said we was to clear off and stop spreading rumour.

May　Quite right.

Bertha　But everyone's going up and down, round and round, they'll go out of their minds. Who's that over there? Sarah? No. All the nurses have been stopped their leave, have you heard? Jessie Bains had only just got home and there was a bobby round at their home with an order for her to go back. She'd only time for a cup of tea and she was back on the train. Listen! There's people shouting down the hill. People running.

Sarah (*off*)　Bertha!

Bertha　Sarah!

Sarah *runs on, white and breathless. During what she says* **Eva** *will enter quietly, to one side.*

Sarah   Seven ... seven ... there's only seven of them left. The Pals. Only seven left alive. Out of nearly seven hundred men.

Bertha   Oh no God ... don't ... don't ...

Sarah   We talked to the railwaymen that had been at Manchester Central. There's crowds there trying to find out what they can from the drivers and people coming from London. Well apparently it's certain because down in London they've spoken with stretcher bearers that crossed with the wounded yesterday into Dover. They asked them were any from up here. They said there were wounded Manchesters but there were not likely to be any Accringtons for they were wiped out ... except for seven.

May   How could they know for sure?

Sarah   They were there! They still had the dirt and mess on their uniforms. And there was a young officer. He said he wasn't supposed to confirm it ... but he did. And he was a big well-spoken young man but he was crying.

Eva   They treat us like children but we'll not behave like children. D'you believe it now May? I've been thinking and talking to one or two up the street. There's a general opinion that we should force them to tell us properly at the Town Hall. And we should all go there in the morning and make sure they do. And I mean everybody. Will you two go round with me and knock on doors?

Sarah   Yes. That's good. Bertha and me'll do all Waterloo Street if you like ...

Bertha   I couldn't ...

Sarah   You can! We'll get that bloody Mayor stood in front of us and if he says he doesn't know he can get on his

telephone to wherever and find out! We'll march there!
Come on Bertha. Let's get started.

Bertha   If only they could be alive!

Sarah *leads her away.*

Eva   You'll come with us May –

May   No!

Eva   D'you still not believe it?

May   I believe what I believe.

Eva   Will you let yourself believe that Tom's one of the
seven?

May   I shall find out myself.

Eva   How? That's what we're going for.

May   Marching!

Eva   We're going together, that's all.

May   They should make up their own minds ...

Eva   They will. It's little enough we're asking. We just want
to know. For all of us.

May   If Tom's hurt ... if they've hurt him ... I'll find out.
And I'll find out for myself.

Eva *goes.* **May** *stands stock still and after some moments calls softly.*

May   Tom ... Tom ...

*Into her imagination comes the sound of guns in a series of faint
echoes. The stage darkens. A flare going off in the distance bathes the
edge of the stage in white light. It fades.* **Reggie** *runs on.*

Reggie   Did you see it miss? Did you?

May   What?

Reggie   Lights in the sky. We've seen three from back
kitchen up over the moors. I thought it were a Zeppelin

on fire. Mother saw it. Her thinks it's to light the way from
France. Thinks it's the Germans burning the moor. That
they've killed all our soldiers and they're coming through ...
she's real bad. I'm sent for doctor.

Getting no response from **May** *he goes. She stares at the sky.*

May Where? Where?

*She rushes to the stall and closes the tarpaulin. She crosses forward
on the darkened stage looking for lights.*

Tom ... shall I dare to look at you? Are you crawling? Are
you breathing?

*A louder burst of machine-gun fire. She jumps back against the
tarpaulin.*

Where's those lights? I want to see you. I'm not scared ...
they're the ones who are scared. Afraid to stand on their
own!

A flare. **CSM Rivers** *enters.*

Rivers That's the spirit, miss.

May You!

Rivers I always admired your spirit.

May Where's Tom?

Rivers Near. You're with the Pals.

May Show me Tom.

Rivers He'll come to you. You've brought yourself so far.
He'll come.

May He's alive!

Rivers In my care.

A flare. **May** *cowers.*

Rivers Stand up Miss Hassal. Nothing'll reach you here.

May   Oh the stench!

Rivers   A bit ripe. A bit gamey. And Fritz don't help, stirring up the offal.

May   Will Tom be here soon?

Rivers   They all will. He'll report here.

May   But they said only seven were left!

Rivers   Seven? That's a rumour number. There's only five hundred and eighty-five dead or wounded ... and that leaves near a hundred. Not so bad as your West Yorks or Tynesiders.

May   Which way are the Germans?

Rivers   Up there.

May   Give me that rifle.

Rivers   Well you are a Tartar. Could you use it?

May   Show me.

Rivers   I'm honoured, Miss Hassal. But not in anger or hate. That only upsets the aim. Kneel. Thighs braced apart but easy.

He holds the rifle in position. She presses the butt to her shoulder.

Not against the collarbone. Just under it there's a pad of flesh that God provided for the convenience of riflemen. Nurse it to you. Twist your arm in the sling, so. Take the weight.

May   It's heavy!

Rivers   As a lover ... that being my fancy to say to the men and remind them what comforts them most in the presence of death ... for fear, like anger and hate, make a bad rifleman. Look along the barrel to the tip of the fore-sight ... which it is my whim to call the male ... for as you

see, the back sight is a slit ... open and ready to receive.
Bring the one gently to the other ... Have they touched?

May   Yes.

Rivers   When I say so take a short breath for the count of
two. No longer or you'll begin to waver. Understood?

May   Yes.

Rivers   When you see your target, which I call the object of
desire ...

Tom *enters, shadowy.*

May (*sensing him*)   There! There!

Rivers   Make a moment of calm and ... squeeze the trigger
lovingly!

She fires at the shadowy figure. **Tom** *raises his head, as though the
shot raised a memory. His face is the face of a corpse.*

May   Tom!

Rivers   I said he'd come to you.

May   Tom!

Rivers   Keep away. They spit like toads some of them. He'd
tear the inside from your body if he could. Look at his eyes.

May   But it's Tom ...

Rivers   Don't insult him by putting his name to that! None
of us would want our names put to what we are in the first
few hours of death. All we are then is what we spew up in
our last belch. Blind panic, vengeance, and terror ... that's
all we are at first. Flying off the battlefield screaming like
starlings. It's all a poor soldier can do to fling himself down
on the earth and cling on to life with his bleeding fingertips
till they've sailed by freezing the skin up his back. But our
Tom was a hero. He saw his good friends die, the old one
refusing God, the young one shot, his head puffed up blue
as a sugar bag as the bullet went through. You went fighting

mad didn't you boy? Waving his rifle at that flock of ghosts – all shrieking and chirping. Ah ... he remembers.

May   Tom! It's May ...

Tom *leaps back, snarling.*

Rivers   Come on boy. This is Miss Hassal. Speak love to him. Pity him. Tell him he should have a medal. That's what he wants to hear. He's full of envy that someone else is alive, d'ye see?

May (*to* **Tom**)   I should have loved you ...

Rivers   Don't say that. Tell him he died a hero.

May   He died a slave!

Rivers   He died a soldier, with his brothers in arms ...

May   No! He was alone. In the end you're on your own. I told him time and time again. It's hard. It's unbearable. But you've got to believe it! If only he'd stood up for himself and not let himself be led ... then I shouldn't have killed him.

Rivers   You? Hear that boy? Why the one that did that was some little pot-bellied Woortenberger ... some pint-sized sausage eater, wasn't he boy? Stood up on his parapet thinking all the Tommies were wiped out ... then sees this madcap scarecrow ripping his way out of the wire. Bang! Tom's dead.

Tom *has begun to grin at the memory.*

Tom   We exchanged our skills. No money was involved ...

May   Slave! If you hadn't died like one you'd have lived like one. Oh this stench! This stink!

Rivers   Come on Hackford. Up!

May   Your words ... your dreams ... your promised lands ... your living for others ... none of it would have saved you!

Rivers   Get fell in!

May   You'd have groused and grumbled about your dunderheads and numbskulls ... but all the same when they opened their cage to you you'd have walked right in and locked the door. They'd have taken everything and all the love in the world would have made no difference.

Rivers   Up with the others on the road. Move!

May   No! I want you to condemn me ...

She reaches out her hands to **Tom**.

I sat there ... and I thought it would be better if you didn't come back.

Tom *stares at her hands. A memory of life stirs in him. He reaches out and gently touches them.* **May** *feels the cold strike through her.*

Rivers   Get on parade Hackford! Fall in you happy warriors! Get fell in the Pals! Move yourselves you glorious dead!

We hear the parade. Marching begins. **May**, *staring in horror at her hands, retreats to the stall and sits. Lights fade to blackout.*

Scene Eight

Lights come up on **May** *sitting by the stall.* **Reggie** *enters. He pauses.* **May** *doesn't look up.*

Reggie   Shall I take covers back, miss?

She nods. He begins to tie the sheets back.

Her's more settled now. Mother.

May   Oh is she? Good.

Reggie   They say rest. Just rest. Sorry I didn't come to unpack last night miss. Shall I get the onions?

He waits for a reply but gets none.

Enter **Eva** *with a suitcase and more or less the same belongings she came with at the beginning of the play.* **Reggie** *looks from one to the other.*

Eva   I wasn't sure you'd got my address written down anywhere so I've left it propped up on the mantel shelf.

Reggie   Shall I get the onions?

Eva *nods. He goes.*

Eva   He can do the stall on his own now. You don't have to sit out here.

May   It's funny ... I've been staring at the backs of my hands and they look very peculiar. Shiny and a bit shrivelled. But then I can't remember when I last looked at them properly. Will your sister want you there long?

Eva   Yes. I've told you. She's at her wits' end. They can scarcely do much at all for themselves. Father's quite incapable.

May   I need you to put me right. You seem to know instinctively. You were right about going to Town Hall, weren't you? And the Mayor took it very well ... sending to the War Office to find out ... Oh ... I had such a beautiful letter from Tom's aunt in Salford. (*Puzzled.*) Did I ... show it you?

Eva   Yes. May, I'm going.

May   Shall we ask Reggie to get the cart and wheel your things to the stop?

Eva   It's all right. Sarah and Bertha are waiting to walk along with me.

May   Oh yes. 1 won't come then.

Eva   May, you're welcome to come!

May   No, I don't think I will. But I would like you to do one little thing for me. It was just something in the paper yesterday. That man who writes the poems ... I expect you saw it.

Eva   Yes.

May (*getting the paper from the stall*)   You read things so well. Would you?

Eva   Oh May ... don't ask me ...

May   Please. I'd like to hear it read.

Eva *takes the paper reluctantly.*

Eva
'There are tear-dimmed eyes in the town today,
There are lips to be no more kissed ...'

Reggie *enters with the basket.* **May** *motions him to stand still.*

May   Just a moment, Reggie.

The sight of the two of them waiting for her to continue increases **Eva***'s anger with the situation.*

Eva
    'There are bosoms that swell with an aching heart
    When they think of their dear ones missed.
    But time will ...' (*Breaks off*)
    I don't know this word. I don't know it.

But **May** *still waits patiently.* **Eva** *is forced to continue.*

'But time will ...' something ...

May   'Assuage ...'

Eva
    '   their heartfelt grief
    Of their sons they will proudly tell
    How in gallant charge in the world wide war
    As Pals they fought and fell.'

She hands back the paper to **May** *with:*

It doesn't say what I feel. Makes me angry.

May   Well, you can't put everything in one poem.

Eva   Bye May. Bye Reggie.

Eva *goes.* **Reggie** *puts the basket on the stall.*

May   Oh those are good onions. You have done well. I shall have to start paying you more.

Bugle band.

Questions and Activities

1. One reviewer, commenting on the realistic and 'dream-like' sequences in the play, thought that they 'sit uneasily together'. Do you agree?
2. Whelan, in his preface to the first edition of the play, wrote that the play 'poses the eternal double-edged question: how much am I for others and how much am I for myself?' In what ways do you think this question applies to the play?
3. Dominic Dromgoole has commented that 'Peter Whelan dives into history, digs deep, and comes up with small stories, pearls fashioned by the grit of life, that illuminate then and now.' Given the period of the writing of the play, in what ways does it illuminate both 'then' and 'now'?
4. 'May is not always popular with locals – but she attracts the sympathy of the audience.' Do you think this is true? Why or why not?
5. Unusually for a male writer the female characters are drawn more strongly than the male. Do you agree?
6. 'We are all crossing No Man's Land now.' This was the last sentence of Peter Whelan's original introduction to the play. In what senses are any of the characters in the play doing this?
7. To what extent can it be said that this is a play about survival?
8. In most plays at least one of the characters has a 'journey' – that is, they change, progress or come to a realisation. Which characters have 'journeys' in this play? And which is the most significant 'journey'?
9. CSM Rivers is the only true 'outsider' in the play. What is his dramatic function in the play and is the play the better for his presence in it?

10. For a specific theatre that you know, create a set design for the play which will both reflect the play's period and style and enable a fluid production.
11. Consider the ways in which theatre technology (sound, lights, special effects) would enhance a production of the play. Use as a basis the existing stage directions.
12. Imagine that you are May just after the end of the play. Write a diary entry, trying to be honest about the feelings which your experiences have left you with.
13. Imagine that you are Eva just after the end of the play. Write two letters – one to May, looking back on their experiences and one to Ralph (he's dead of course, but she wants to express her feelings and thoughts to him).
14. Imagine that you are a reporter from the *Accrington Observer*. You have been told to interview the women at the end of the play, either individually or in pairs/groups. Improvise and/or write these interviews.
15. Choose points from the past history of the relationship between May and Tom to construct a series of improvisations between them, showing the developments and changes in their relationship. Remember that there is a ten-year age gap between them. Use the information which the play gives you as a basis.